PRAISE

"Customer service has been around forever, yet many companies fail to provide quality service to their customers. By creating a pattern of excellence, Brigham's book applies common knowledge principles and turns them into common practice."

—**JEFFREY HAYZLETT,** primetime TV and podcast show host, keynote speaker, best-selling author, and global business celebrity

"The book is introspective, thoughtful, and sewn together with a cord of servant leadership from start to finish. It is a book you will want to read for yourself, buy for your team, and give to your children."

—**MATT MICHEL,** President of Service Nation Inc., Contracting Business Hall of Fame

"*Patterned after Excellence* will help your company become a model of success and prosperity. Read this book, and implement its leadership and service principles. You and your business deserve excellence. This book will teach you how to get there."

—**WELDON LONG,** author of *The Upside of Fear*, *Consistency Selling*, and *The Power of Consistency*, a *New York Times* and *Wall Street Journal* bestseller

"*Patterned after Excellence* makes a compelling case for accepting the challenge of shifting your focus from serving yourself to serving others. Brigham's stories about his company, employees, and their successful journeys to help their customers thrive and grow by adopting a true sense of purpose and living the simple truths he shares make it clear: It's not hard to prioritize serving others, but it takes vigilance and discipline to stay the course."

—**MIKE HART,** Vice President of Residential Sales at Lennox Industries

"This book is inspirational, real, deep and had an impact on how I see myself, my business, and my life."

—**ARA MAHDESSIAN,** CEO of ServiceTitan

"A timely and ambitious book on leadership and self improvement. You are the enemy. You can be the hero. Stop blaming, and start leading!"

—**VAHE KUZOYAN,** President and Co-Founder of ServiceTitan

"What a timely book! Brigham combines personal experience and common-ground truths to transcend our diverse human beliefs, pinpointing, in great detail, those human tendencies that keep us from winning life's pivotal moments. Once I started reading, I couldn't put the book down. For leaders and those who want to be, this is a *must*-read!"

—**ELLEN ROHR,** COO of Zoom Franchise Company; Business Makeover Coach at Bare Bones Biz; columnist for the *Huffington Post*; Ziglar Legacy Certified Trainer

"In his new book, Brigham has managed to address the specific challenges we are facing through the timeless application of first-principle thinking. You will want to read this book and then get all of your team a copy and keep it handy."

—**EDWARD MCFARLANE,** VP of Learning and Development at Haller Enterprises, Inc.

"Brigham Dickinson's *Patterned after Excellence* is moving. First, you will move through profound insights for your own journey, realizing how you can improve your business even in the first few pages, as this book weaves motivation, proven business success, and spirituality unlike most books can. Then, from Brigham's own hall-of-fame-worthy sales strategies, his life experiences and the examples of legends from the past. This book will change your life and your business in a read you won't be able to put down. The concepts in every chapter will ignite your own immediate excellence. Read this book now to find your Truth, your unique-to-you Human Tendency, and create your own Winning Moments!"

—**JASON HEWLETT,** CSP, CPAE Speaker Hall of Fame, leadership expert, author of *Signature Moves*

"The start-up life is not for the faint of heart, and despite the lowest moments and valleys of despair, I've done it 3 times in the past 15 years. Were it not for the exact principles Brigham Dickinson outlines in this inspirational book, my start-up success would only be a dream. His Pattern of Excellence is a valuable playbook for any motivated person with serious life and business goals."

—**JAY BEAN,** CEO of FreshLime

PATTERNED
After
EXCELLENCE

PURSUING TRUTH *in* WORK *and* LIFE

BRIGHAM DICKINSON

Foreword by James Lawrence

RIVER GROVE
BOOKS

This publication is designed to provide accurate and authoritative information in regard to the subject matter covered. It is sold with the understanding that the publisher and author are not engaged in rendering legal, accounting, or other professional services. Nothing herein shall create an attorney-client relationship, and nothing herein shall constitute legal advice or a solicitation to offer legal advice. If legal advice or other expert assistance is required, the services of a competent professional should be sought.

Published by River Grove Books
Austin, TX
www.rivergrovebooks.com

Distributed by River Grove Books

Design and composition by Greenleaf Book Group
Cover design by Greenleaf Book Group
Cover image: ©iStockphoto.com/Olivier Le Moal
Author photo by Daisy Tree Photography

Publisher's Cataloging-in-Publication data is available.

Paperback ISBN: 978-1-63299-234-5

Hardcover ISBN: 978-1-63299-256-7

eBook ISBN: 978-1-63299-235-2

First Edition

" . . . there is no truth more thoroughly established, than that there exists [. . .] an indissoluble union between virtue and happiness . . . "

—GEORGE WASHINGTON

CONTENTS

ENDURANCE

A s the title says, this is a book about excellence, truth, human tendency, and winning moments. But it's also a book about another concept: *endurance.*

Reading, understanding, and acting on what Brigham Dickinson lays out here requires endurance—constant effort, discipline, determination, and hard work. Success will require undauntedly striving through all of life's ups and downs: rejection, heartaches, injustices, sorrow, insensitivity, loss, poverty, weakness, aloneness, disasters, unresponsiveness, physical illness and pain, mental and emotional anguish, unjust criticism, moments of being misunderstood, and unfair, unreasonable, or undeserved representations. Excellence is measured by how you respond to these things and by how well you realize that you have the capacity to outlast, stand firm against, and suffer through them when they happen—sometimes all at once. In other words, you must come to realize that you can endure.

And I know a bit about that. When I announced my plan to complete fifty full-distance triathlons in fifty consecutive days in fifty states, the only people who believed in me were my wife and kids. Swim, bike, and run 140.6 miles every day in every state? I get it. It sounds crazy, even for someone like me, who had already set endurance records. But I endured, and it is now called by many the single greatest feat in human endurance history.

How did I get there? In 2010 I set a Guinness World Record by completing twenty-two half Ironmans in one year. Then, in 2012 I was on the verge of setting another record, having just finished twenty-eight of thirty Ironmans that year, and I felt . . . empty. I had not reached or truly tested my physical and mental limits. That's when it popped into my head: 50/50/50. I bought the biggest map of the United States I could find and started to draw route lines on it with my kids.

But that's not where my choice to pattern my life after excellence began. It started for me in 2008, when I was doing well working in the mortgage industry and the market collapsed. A seemingly safe job disappeared, and the good life I had built for my family was threatened, if not already gone. My response? Play it safe. My whole life, I had been told to stay in the safe lane, so I took a safe job after the market downturn and almost lost myself in the process. That's when I made the choice to stop chasing the dream others had told me to pursue and to go after mine.

In moments of great adversity, you show the others what kind of person you really are. Will you fight for what you want and finish what you start? Or will you react with fear and give in to the worst human tendencies—forgetting who you are and losing yourself in the process? When tragedy, disappointment, and heartache affect our lives, it's easy to become self-centered and resentful of others instead of opening up and pushing forward to reach our potential—going further than we ever thought and then continuing to push for excellence. That's endurance.

During my 50/50/50, I survived internal bleeding, hypothermia, hyperthermia, dehydration, nerve damage, tropical storms, infected foot blisters, and a blood-clot scare. I suffered from extreme sleep deprivation and fell asleep on my bike on day eighteen. The pain from the resulting crash would linger months after I finished. Yet in many ways enduring the naysayers (especially on social media) was worse: These people questioned my sanity and accused me of keeping the funds we raised for charity. The emotional strain had me thinking about quitting until I remembered my wife and kids, and what it meant to them and the people I knew I was helping. This wasn't about me. I stopped feeling sorry for myself. I was going to finish no matter what. With my mind set, my body adapted to the pain enough that I could finish what I set out to do.

Endurance is not about taking a beating; it's about gaining strength from it. This mind-set was critical to my finishing the 50/50/50 and will be critical to whatever your life's 50/50/50 will be. Without it, you cannot endure the path Brigham sets out in this book, let alone the one to excellence. All the things he asks us to do, such as being optimistic, having confidence without ego, listening to and caring about others, and understanding what it means to live in truth, are impossible unless you have the right mind-set to win the moments that matter.

You cannot achieve what Brigham calls *a life patterned after excellence* without something bigger than you driving you forward. Find it, and let it drive your 50/50/50. Fight for it. Hold on to it! Endure it, and you will find joy that too few pay the price to experience in this life.

James Lawrence

Author of *Iron Cowboy: Redefine Impossible*

2018

HEARTS MATTER MORE THAN WALLETS

I was lying awake, stuck in my head, staring at nothing, and thinking about everything I held dear. The morning had brought the realization that my life and livelihood were on the line. Five months earlier, I had moved my family to Florida from Utah to merge my marketing company with a software company there. I thought it was going to go gangbusters and it went . . . kaput.

Now here I was with four kids and a wife, stuck in both a state of mind and a state I had no business or prospects in. I looked at my cell phone lying on the ground. The night before, I had thrown it there after talking with a mentor and close friend. He had offered me money to help make ends meet. I should have accepted the money, but my pride got in the way. I graciously declined and hung up before a feeling of worthlessness overwhelmed me, and I took it out on the phone. It was so overpowering that I could not stand up. I stumbled across my bedroom floor, fell to my knees, and cried like I had never cried before.

I thought back to when I had asked my father-in-law for his daughter's hand in marriage. I was in college and had a meager income. He asked how I was going to take care of her, and I promised him I would find a way. And I had—until now. For ten years, we had never had a problem with money. Now we did, and I watched our marriage begin to disintegrate as we dealt with stresses we had never dealt with before, doing our best to hide it from the kids. I know that for many, the "bottom" looks a lot worse, but mine hurt badly and sapped me of my confidence. I needed to get it back and right my sinking ship.

With my company hanging by the thread of a few clients, I kissed my family goodbye in Florida, drove back to Utah, crashed on a cot in my brother-in-law's basement, and set out to rebuild my business. One of the few clients I had was a plumbing and heating company that was about to fire me because their call handlers were not booking leads that came in from our ads. The company was losing money and potential customers by the day as its handlers struggled in every situation—whether someone just wanted a price, needed an appointment sooner than my client could help, or simply took the information and said, "I'll call back."

I knew why my client wasn't booking calls: There was no magic in the conversations with customers, no connection between the call handlers and the callers. Each call needed to feel like the start of a relationship, not a transaction—it needed to be not about the price but about the customer's experience. Hearts had to matter more than wallets.

Looking for inspiration to change my attitude, restore my confidence, and help all my clients so I could rebuild my company, I turned to business, self-help, and history books for inspiration. I filled journals with ideas that soon formed the foundation of a tool to help my clients stop thinking about themselves and become present in the moment when their customers call. I called this tool the *Pattern for Excellence*—a framework for learning best practices in phenomenal customer service. It also became the title of my first book, *Pattern for Excellence: Engage Your Team to WOW More Customers.*

PATTERN FOR EXCELLENCE

If you look at the Pattern for Excellence and think, *There's nothing new here*, you're right! People who read my previous book or encounter the Pattern for Excellence for the first time often say something like "Well, I know these things. Everybody knows these things."

But knowing and acting on that knowledge are two very different things. While the Pattern for Excellence is based on common knowledge, it is not *common practice*. You must *practice* these principles—not just know them—over and over again, and apply them consistently. This works in customer service for sure, but even more importantly, it works in life.

If you're staying awake at night wanting to book more calls or close more sales, then you're staying awake at night for the wrong reasons. Did your customer have a good experience working with you? Would he or she do business with you again? These are the questions that should be keeping you up at night. They are the questions that the Pattern for Excellence helps you learn to ask and answer. Being present in the moment allows you to listen to, care for, and reassure others. You can ask the right questions, find out what is missing, and create valuable solutions for them. Only then will you create better experiences for those you serve.

Mastery of the Pattern for Excellence and its principles is a journey that empowers your company, your employees, and you to achieve at a higher level.

★ You become more aware and persuasive in your communication.

★ You get more done in less time.

★ You are better able to work with others.

★ You create *Wow!* experiences for your customers and everyone you work with.

Again, this customer-experience-focused business model is easy to say but hard to achieve for one primary reason: It's so easy to get sidetracked by the numbers. Dollars and cents distract us from the people we are serving. By focusing more on connecting with others—your customers, your employees, your vendors—you and your team will create trust and loyalty with each other and the customers you serve.

That's how you build long-term relationships: You learn to serve others, not sell to them. Price matters less to them because of the value you've created through this connection. As you serve your customers, striving to constantly exceed their expectations, a whole new world of customer loyalty opens up. If customers like you and continue to like you, they have a positive emotional connection to you—not just a transactional one. They are therefore much more likely to continue doing business with you and recommend your services to their friends.

The proof that this pattern and its principles work is in the results. I knew from my experience with my client that it was not enough to tell their call handlers to provide better customer service; I needed to *teach* them how to do it. It required a lot of practice on their part once I set the expectation for what I was looking to hear as I listened to their calls and evaluated their progress over time. As we helped them master the eight principles in the pattern, the call handlers created connections with their callers and provided that customer-focused experience. A year after I created the Pattern for Excellence, I had used it not only to save that plumbing and heating client but to transform my business into a small training company that taught customer service representatives how to better handle incoming calls.

LIVING TRUTH

Through the Pattern for Excellence, not only did my clients increase sales, but my reborn company doubled in size every year for four years straight. Things were going great. Then our growth plateaued for a year. Then two. This lack of growth wore on me, and I started losing confidence again. I began to feel alone and fearful of the future. And just like during that call from my mentor five years earlier, pride got in the way of my asking for help until it was almost too late. By the time I did ask someone and hired a business consultant named Johnny Covey, we were more than two years into stagnant growth, and I was ready to call it quits.

I'm glad I didn't, because the solution to the problem was as simple as practicing what I preached. After a company meeting in which

I drilled my employees on booking calls, closing sales, and handling collections, Johnny helped me realize that I had failed to address the principles I teach my clients in the Pattern for Excellence. We were teaching our clients to make the transition from a money-driven, transactional business to a customer-experience-focused business in their workplaces, but we weren't doing the same in ours!

I had unwittingly stopped implementing the very tool that helped so many of my clients grow their businesses and improve their company culture. I was not living by the principles—the universal truths—that I knew worked for others. A verse from the Bible immediately echoed in my mind: "But be ye doers of the word, and not hearers only, deceiving your own selves" (KJV, James 1:22). I had been blind to my world, myself, and the workings of my very own company!

That day, the Pattern for Excellence evolved from a tool I used to help my clients realize a set of truths that our organization lives by in all our hiring, training, and firing processes. It made me a better leader. It made all of us more capable in our responsibilities. Mastery of these principles has given everyone at the company a great sense of purpose. We avoid selfish and self-defeating tendencies that can keep us from winning interpersonal moments. Our workplace is now filled with contagious positive energy! It is a continuous flow of input and sharing, not gossip or side talk that creates silos, fueling office politics. In every department, the atmosphere and culture of our workplace is about maintaining that excellence. I have a team of individuals with great customer-centric ideas, and it is my responsibility to help them develop those ideas, because when they come to fruition, they will benefit all of us, especially our clients.

As a result, our company went from stagnant growth to tripling its size, all because we got over ourselves and went to work thinking more about our customers than ourselves. We began to live by the truths we teach: the principles found in the Pattern for Excellence.

PATTERN *AFTER* EXCELLENCE

A decade later, the tool I created after I hit bottom is still improving my life and the lives of those with whom I work and interact. But I was also only beginning to understand how deep it could go. I have come to discover an even more elevated purpose for the Pattern for Excellence: By applying its principles, I have also become a better father and husband—a better *person*—not just a better boss.

Simply put, the Pattern for Excellence and its principles are universal truths that work every time when correctly applied in each and every aspect of life. But this realization was not immediate. It is a journey to living a life patterned *after* excellence.

The Pattern for Excellence provides eight segments of successful interaction, and behind each of these is a universal truth. In *Pattern after Excellence*, each chapter highlights a human tendency that undermines our acceptance of one of those truths. These tendencies keep us from winning meaningful moments, but I believe if we overcome them and accept reality, we will experience greater joy and more meaning in what we do. In other words, there is a way out: choosing to live a life patterned after excellence.

CHAPTER 1

YOUR OWN WORST ENEMY

A t the beginning of my son Isaac's wrestling season, he and I were among the first to show up at a planned trail run with Coach Garcia and all the kids on the team. Coach Garcia and his two boys arrived early as well, and while we were waiting for the other boys to show up, Coach's sons began to taunt me a little bit, confident that their dad could beat me on this trail. I have never been one for smack talk. Instead, I let it ignite an adrenaline-fueled response. They were just kids, so I was doing a pretty good job at keeping it all in proper perspective until they told Isaac what they told me. As I heard them say, "My dad could beat your dad," I took one look at Coach Garcia, and it was on.

On paper, Coach Garcia and I were evenly matched. Both of us are in our early forties and in good shape, and we know the trail well: five miles long, with five hundred feet of elevation gain up the mountain. We had never raced each other before, so I started at the back of the pack and let Coach Garcia lead the front. I wanted him to set the pace so I could see how hard he would push the boys. I assumed (correctly) that he would not pull too far away from them. Once the pace was set, I made my move. Coach Garcia never saw me coming. I started passing kids on the first steep incline and sprinted past him until I was about twenty-five feet in front. I set my pace and settled in for what I thought would be an easy four and a half miles to the finish line.

That is, until I came around the second corner where the trail zig-zagged up the mountain. I could see that Coach Garcia had closed the gap to ten feet behind me.

I leaned forward to pick up my pace, determined to stay in front as we scaled the mountain. I was confident that if I sped up to a near-sprint for about fifty yards, Coach Garcia would lose his nerve and slow down. This would give me an opportunity to slow down as well and catch my breath. But as I sprinted around the next turn, he was still there, ten feet behind me. Sure, he was working visibly harder than I was, but that made him look more angry than tired.

A mile and a half into the race, I reached the top and could see the rest of the team half a mile back. Coach Garcia was still ten feet behind me.

I shifted my body weight back a little as I transitioned into the descent with wide leaping strides, letting my heels strike the ground first as I tried to catch my breath. I should have taken short, choppy steps like I did coming up the hill and let the balls of my feet hit the ground first, but I was too tired. Coming around the second downhill bend, I looked up and saw that I was finally pulling away. I reached the turnaround point at the bottom of the other side and quickly doubled back up the mountain for the last mile-long incline. Shifting my weight forward on my toes, my quads began to burn—the painful backlash of sprinting almost nonstop up the first mile and a half of the mountain. My pace slowed a little.

That's when Coach Garcia passed me on his descent down the hill. He smiled as he flew by me.

"Good job, Brigham," he said as he passed.

"You too, Coach. Nice run," I responded, doing my best to hide my irritation and the feeling in my legs. I didn't have much left. There was no way I could do what I did on the first mile and a half.

Then, suddenly, Coach Garcia was ten feet behind me again. As I climbed with all my might, I realized the only reason I made it up the first incline ahead of him was because he was saving his legs for the second run up the mountain. I was not the only one with a strategy. He may have outwitted me on the second incline, but he was still going to have to catch me. I just had to stay in front, I thought. No matter what, just stay in front.

The chase continued all the way up the hill. Isaac and one of Coach Garcia's sons had both just barely reached the top of the first incline. They greeted me and then Coach, who was now only a few feet behind. As soon as I hit the top and shifted my weight for the final descent, I could feel him on my heels. He was trying to pass me. I widened my stride, leaping as far as I could with each step down the hill while avoiding catching a rock and taking a horrific fall. On the sketchy, steep cutbacks, I took quick, short steps on the balls of my feet so I could maintain speed without tripping or sliding. If he was going to pass me, he'd have to earn it. And I had no intention of letting him do that. *I was going to beat him.*

I laughed out loud as I found new energy and strength. With a half mile left, I took a sharp right down the trail and heard Coach Garcia slip and fall right behind me. I thought that was it. But he popped up almost as quickly as he fell, ignoring his scraped-up right thigh. I pushed myself even harder.

The last quarter mile was the fastest I had ever run. I crossed the finish line thirty seconds ahead of Coach Garcia. When our boys finally finished, they asked who won. I said, "We both did."

Coach then responded, "Nah, he did."

Coach's boys were dumbfounded. Isaac smiled, and his smile made me smile.

According to his stopwatch, my time was two minutes faster than I had ever run that trail. I had no idea that kind of speed was in me in my forties. I had competed as if I were going after a gold medal.

That's just it, though: I wasn't going after a gold medal. I was there to support my son and his wrestling teammates. It wasn't supposed to be a race; it was supposed to be a run—exercise and team building. My son might have been smiling, but I knew I had let him down. I had let Coach Garcia down, too, and I had let the team down. Did my actions support my son's team by leaving my son and his teammate behind? Did I inspire confidence in their coach by goading him into a silly contest? It was supposed to be about the team, and I made it about me. I wasn't the hero of this story; I was the enemy—my own worst enemy.

UNIVERSAL TRUTH

Universal truth should not be confused with individual belief. When people refer to a belief as "their" truth, as if they own it, they are simply stating a personal belief that appeals to them; that doesn't make it a reality. For example, even though you may wholeheartedly believe that an apple seed you plant in your backyard will one day become a beautiful apricot tree, natural laws will prevent your desired outcome from occurring. In other words, when "your truth" flies in the face of universal truth—natural laws, what consequently happens as a result of individual action, independently of your belief—the stark difference between "your truth" and what is universally true becomes more apparent.

When we pit what we feel is our truth against what is universally true, we only deceive ourselves. Why? Because the consequences may not match our expectations. Consequences occur independently of what we feel or believe. When we betray what is universally true, we'll quickly come to realize in a pivotal moment that we also betray our true selves. This self-deception also keeps others from seeing who we are, which betrays and deprives them also. Our ability to change ourselves—and live a life patterned after excellence—depends on facing that truth and confronting those self-betrayals.

In my case, the truth I betrayed on that hill came down to my inability to recognize that it wasn't a race. It wasn't about me! It was about my son and his team. It was neither the time nor the place to show up Coach Garcia or his boys. My true self—the best me, the person I yearn to be—loves my son and wanted to serve and support him, but I let my ego rule the day as selfishness took its toll on my actions.

Thinking only about yourself serves no one. I should have known this before I ran that "race," and I should have stopped myself from acting the way I did.

I also should have recognized this human tendency to act selfishly before I let my business struggle and fail so many years ago. But the inflexible truth is always hard to face openly and honestly. And once we get where we want to be, able to choose what is right instead of what is natural or easy in a given moment, we don't remain there without constant personal work. The process is often painful, but as long as we avoid turning bitter or prideful as we pass through trials, our wins and losses can make us stronger than we were before. The struggle we feel as we face our worst tendencies and overcome them acts as a metamorphosis, shifting us into entirely different creatures.

When we discover the truth, we can embrace it, living as our most authentic selves. When we stay true to ourselves, we begin to live with purpose. We free ourselves from circumstance and negative consequences. No matter what happens, we become and remain who we were always meant to be. We have found our true selves.

You have to discover yourself on your own. We do not arrive in this life fully formed; we are born knowing nothing about ourselves. We know we came from our parents, and we know we are free to choose how we respond to circumstances as they occur. The rest is up to us.

But in our youthful ignorance, we tend to hold on to identities that simply aren't true. They are stories we tell about ourselves or let others write for us. In high school, I told myself I wasn't a good reader. Then

I made it true. I was labeled by others as hyper and unable to focus. I chose to believe that too. But I was not actually a bad reader, and I was not all that hyper compared to many kids. These were identities I adopted that held me back from growing.

Most of us have similar stories: You were told something or told yourself something that you chose to believe, impeding your ability to actualize your full and true identity. The only one who is holding you back is yourself.

★

HIGHER AUTHORITY

A few years back, I attended a business conference featuring Simon Sinek, of *Start with Why* and TED Talk fame. Sinek may be the person most responsible for millions upon millions of leaders inspiring action and living with purpose. After he spoke, I had the opportunity to ask him a question: "As I've read your books, I can't help but wonder, do you believe in a Creator?"

Sinek's response was extremely profound and a wise testament to the importance of living truths:

> *I'm completely agnostic as to how our existence came to be. In other words, for me, the responsibilities I have and the cause I adhere to every day is that we care about each other. And the organizations we build are responsible for the people who serve inside our organizations. . . . Whenever anything goes right or goes wrong, I look to the human beings. What we do know is that people who have a sense of spirituality, or a sense of a higher calling, tend to be a lot better at resisting some of the ills that would make people do bad things to each other, because we don't see the authority that*

14

is standing in front of us as the highest authority; we answer to a higher authority. When we answer to a higher authority, a more infinite authority, we are actually much better at making decisions if we always keep that purpose, cause, or belief front and center. All of the best leaders are also the best followers.[1]

Sinek's answer did not dismiss the benefits of believing in a higher authority, whether true or not. He simply focused on what is true about people and relationships. While there is much we have yet to know for certain about life and our grand purpose in it, we do know that we can accomplish much more working together—serving one another regardless of our varying belief systems—than we can alone. History is full of life lessons and replete with this truth, both mistakes to learn from and successes to emulate.

Consider this line carefully: Seek and ye shall find. The process of seeking and finding the truth is a choice, one only you can make. As humans, we are a work in progress. Our resolve must be strong as truth in our lives is discovered, so that new internal practices can be formulated to develop us into what we want to be—or, better yet, what we were meant to be.

For this to happen, we must be open and receptive to change. Constant revision is necessary if we want to move forward. Purpose- and principle-centered living are not for the faint of heart. They require learning by applying, proving, and testing what we know.

As we become strong in our ability to make the choice to overcome human tendencies that hold us back from being our best selves, then apply truth in the service of others, our influence grows. That is what creates winning moments and a life patterned after excellence. As we become strengthened in this excellence, those around us will be strengthened, and our relationships will become all the more endearing and enduring.

★

Even if we convince ourselves that our weaknesses or human tendencies are actually our truth, we will recognize our error as we experience the consequences. This realization also makes caving to human tendency life's only true tragedy. Even though each of us holds the power to follow our own good conscience to create real meaning in our lives by creating meaningful moments for others, we so often choose not to do what we know. Instead, we shrink to mediocrity, disappearing into the crowd of endless sameness and dissolution. It's true: We are often our own worst enemy when it comes to universal truth, but we can be our greatest hero as we seek out, discover, and live by what is universally true.

Here is a universal truth:
We become the best version of ourselves as we serve others.

A life patterned after excellence comes from learning to be consistent with our conscience and the dictates of our own hearts, regardless of what is going on in the world around us. This form of inner peace also cultivates patience, respect, and empathy toward those with different social and political views.

This empathy is the purveyor of a national peace that serves everyone. We can believe different things and yet unite around what matters most: our right to freedom and our families. The choice is ours: Live freely together, or divide and conquer each other until there's nothing left worth fighting for. The real battle is raging between our heads and our hearts, not our fellow men.

The world's greatest teachers, like Dr. Martin Luther King Jr., Gandhi, and even Jesus Christ, have shown us that we can all be individuals and yet serve each other. Dr. King's dream was for a world independent of race or color, a world where people loved one another, treated each other as equals, and were judged by the content of their character, not the color of their skin. Gandhi taught us that we must be the change that we wish to see in the world: For there to be peace in the world, there must first be peace and love in our hearts. Fighting evil with evil helps no one. Christ taught us that we should do good to those who hate us, pray for those who spitefully use us, and love our enemies and not just our neighbors. These are universal truths worth living by.

Those who do not pattern after excellence will live without purpose in their lives. They may become financially well off, but they'll still be left feeling empty and unfulfilled. They will invariably contribute to the problem, turning materialistic, greedy, or self-serving instead of proactively becoming a part of the solution. Simply put, to cultivate peace in the world—especially in the United States— we must first cultivate peace in our hearts by being true to our best selves. To win moments, we must learn to do what we internally know to be right.

For example, let's say you are playing on a golf course with a friendly competitor in your marketplace. While on the ninth hole, your "friend" pulls away to take a phone call. At the same time, you receive a text from an employee informing you that your "friend" is on the phone right now recruiting your best salesperson. This is a pivotal moment. It is a moment where you choose whether to do what is right and act on principle or what is easy and act on emotion. A moment won occurs when you choose to act on what is right based on principle.

OVERCOMING HUMAN TENDENCY

Now you know that you are the one that keeps you from being great and growing. But it is not enough to know this; you must *act* on it. You have to overcome human tendencies such as ego, fear, pride, and so on. For that to happen, you must painstakingly shed your misconceptions—not let past experience, the way you have been portrayed, or your worst tendencies get in your way and define who you are. You must refine the best version of yourself by living according to what is universally true.

That's living a life patterned after excellence. Finding truth and overcoming your human tendencies will help you live in harmony with your conscience and experience a life full of joy in your relationships and accomplishments.

This all comes down to one simple equation:

$$Truth - Human\ Tendency = Winning\ Moments$$

To live by truth, we must stop listening to what we *think* we know or have been conditioned to believe. To overcome human tendency, we must rise above temporary emotions that hold us back, refuse to believe what others may say about us, and stop avoiding the application of hard truths.

BE THE HERO OF YOUR STORY

Moments are the molecules that make up our lives. Most, if not all, moments are won in the service of others. That win usually comes when both you and the one you endeavor to serve—your customer, your employee, your son—walk away from your interaction better off than you were before. In the moment of the race, and so many moments before, I failed to see the bigger picture and live the deeper truths behind the Pattern for Excellence. I ran out in front that day because my pride got in the way.

This realization hit me hard. I had become the enemy of my own story, and I finally understood why. Of course winning is important to achieve excellence. But we must learn to identify those moments when we deceive ourselves and think winning is the *only* thing that matters. Someone else does not have to lose for you to win.

But knowing what you need to do is not enough. Knowledge alone is akin to ignorance until that knowledge is painstakingly replaced with experience. Know-how does not create winning moments; only deeds do. To create winning moments, you must first learn to live by truth rather than human tendency, no matter how much it hurts.

In the face of winning that race, I finally understood what I had to lose in order to truly win: I had to lose the self-centered part of me that stood in the way, that betrayed the truth that defined who I was on a deeper level.

I had failed to overcome my pride, but I was able to see the consequences of my actions. I saw how they had negatively influenced others in my life significantly more than anything I could have said to them. That had to change. I had been my enemy for too long. I had to be the hero of my story and live by truth, absent my worst human tendencies.

Like me, you may be the enemy of your own story. But you can also be the hero. To be the hero, you must learn to overcome your tendencies, discovering and living by universal truth—doing what's right instead of caving to your ego—to create winning moments for other people.

We can all do this. Even though we have been our own worst enemies, we have the power to be heroes and to create winning moments for others. In turn, our true selves share in those winning moments. The human tendency to put ourselves first is powerful and often clouds our judgment. We get stuck in our own heads because of pessimism, ego, forgetfulness, indifference, greed, fear, entitlement, or pride. But none of that matters if we focus on how to turn the situation into a winning moment.

CHAPTER 2

TRUTH AND THE CUSTOMER EXPERIENCE

N ot too long ago, most of us thought business was all about shareholders and the bottom line. It turns out that we were wrong. Most of us know better today, but what are we doing about it aside from paying lip service? Our work must be about others—the customer. If all you do is focus on booking calls, closing sales, and getting the money, you will inevitably let your customers down. It's not just about the numbers. It's not about high-pressure sales. It's not about peddling our products over the phone or otherwise. Stop peddling and start serving.

No business survives without customers, yet the customer experience is one of the most overlooked parts of any business. Simply put, customers want to buy from people and companies they like, and they will like you because of how you make them feel—not because of how much you saved them or the product or service you offered. That may work the first time, but without memorable customer experiences—meaningful, winning moments—the customer will simply have no reason to continue using your company.

When we exceed customer expectations, it is often because we have anticipated their needs, like bringing that free beverage refill before the customer asks for it or fixing an easy additional problem while making the car repair the customer came in for. It also means positive spoken and body language, listening, and a problem-solving mentality—not acting like the people you serve are a necessary evil to be dispensed with quickly or up-sold as much as possible before addressing the problem at hand. Customers experience meaningful moments when they recognize that you went above and beyond in the way you attended to their wants and needs. When a customer says "Wow!" or "How about that!?" it's because you created value for them in unexpected ways and won the moments. These meaningful moments are the outcome you should endeavor to achieve in every human interaction.

The customer experience is often an untapped resource for customer acquisition, independent of the product, service, price, or brand. By providing meaningful moments and customer experiences, you can gain customers without spending money on ads. These customers are effective, free marketing for your business. They are an army of raving fans that will do the work for you: telling their friends just how amazing your company is and posting their experiences on social media. Doesn't this sound more appealing than wasting valuable resources on focus groups or other worn-out marketing strategies just to get the customers' money?

At the end of the day, having a company culture that promotes phenomenal customer experiences also greatly reduces problems within the workplace by creating a "give first" mentality. You and your people are focused less on profit and more on the people you serve to grow your business. You want employees who give maximum effort independent of compensation—independent of how hard the work is or how long it takes. Employees who follow and act upon these true principles of customer experience are the kind of employees every business owner wants in his or her organization.

Companies such as Chick-fil-A and Southwest Airlines pride

themselves on this style of customer interaction. As a result, they have proven that growth can happen when you hold your team to a set of principles, and when you use these principles in your hiring, training, and firing process as well as your customer service. This not only increases productivity and morale but also attracts top talent to your company.

The good news is that by doggedly following a set of true principles in your organization, you can develop and foster results over time. But how do we identify and implement truths to create the highest-functioning business and provide unforgettable customer experiences?

SERVING WITH A PURPOSE

Employees value what you value. If you value money, the same will hold true for your team. Money is a huge motivator for people because it's our livelihood, but it is not the only motivator. In the end, it fails to truly motivate without values or a purpose. Moreover, a business that does not value its customers over profits also does not have any loyalty for its employees. That likely means its employees do not have much loyalty for the company either. They'll chase a bigger payday with another company when the opportunity arises.

If you want to keep your team members and motivate them to put forth their best work in every moment without supervision, they need something beyond money. If you want them to approach their employment with your company as a stewardship, an incredible opportunity to serve others, rather than just another job, then you have to offer them something more than a paycheck. Give them a cause worth fighting for.

A cause-driven business will ensure that your employees are in it for more than the cash. Make sure your organization is about doing some good for others, and let money be a byproduct of that good— not the end goal. You can start now by creating a clear, concise set of values based on the truth you know, so your purpose is evident to both you and your employees in the work you are doing. This is how you'll attract quality employees and endear them to you and your customers.

Genuine customer experiences need to be created consistently over time by your employees. But for them to be willing to make that effort, you have to lead them by example as well as by the expectations you set for them.

★

LIFE IS TOO SHORT FOR "ME"

One Friday evening, my son Isaac asked me to play laser tag. I was tired, so I declined.

"But Dad, you're getting old," he pleaded. "You're running out of time."

Unless my son knew something I did not, death was not knocking on my door at age forty-one, and I aimed to prove that. I grabbed one of the laser guns, and my son went down in a barrage of lasers from his "old man."

After the thumping, I asked Isaac what he meant by what he said. He told me that he didn't know. He had just said it to get me to play with him. Fair enough. Mission accomplished. But I couldn't help asking myself later that evening, *How much time do I have left?* We are all getting older. We are all running out of time. What we're going to do with our unknown amount of time left is the only question.

One of my greatest friends and mentors died a few years ago. I sat and visited with him on his last day. He was not well, but he was still the person I had looked up to for so many years. We exchanged memories. We laughed, reminisced, and shed tears of sadness and joy. We planned to visit the next day, and I went home. Two hours later, I received word that he had passed. Rushing back to his bedside, I saw his body on the bed where we had been talking just a few hours before. He was gone.

> But he left something behind. My mentor had lived by the truth he knew and left that knowledge behind in me. The example he set helped teach me to live by the truth I know. We *all* must do this. By doing so, we will become the leaders our teams and families need us to be.
>
> Choosing to do what is right no matter the circumstance is how you win moments. To teach our team to do this, we must do it ourselves. We came to this life to learn, grow, and strengthen ourselves and our fellow human beings. Learn to be forever present in that truth. Model this for your employees, and they will adopt the same practices. Your business and life will reap the benefits.
>
> ★

CREATING A CAUSE-DRIVEN BUSINESS

Ask yourself what the true purpose of your business is. Once you know the answer, you can begin to consider the steps to align a set of true principles around that cause, and to ensure that those principles are reflected in every employee and customer interaction.

It took me until 2016 to articulate this for myself. I was on the phone with two of my business partners, discussing our concern for the home service industry and for our clients. New players, such as Amazon and Google, had arrived on the scene and were threatening their margins and positions in the marketplace.

Our clients in this industry are nowhere near the size of Amazon; they do $3 to $10 million in annual gross revenue. Many of them have generations-old family businesses (some of them a hundred years old or more). We knew that our clients could not beat Amazon and Google by playing their game. Amazon is a near-trillion-dollar juggernaut. Low price and convenience is their game. Our clients would not beat them trying to do that. The only way they would survive was to provide what Amazon cannot: a unique buying experience. If they did that, they could demand their price and cement—even enlarge—their position in the market. And I realized that our purpose was to train them to do it.

My organization has been teaching customer service since 2008. We know what outstanding customer service looks like, and we know how to teach our clients to consistently win moment after moment in every customer interaction. Why do we succeed? Because it is not about us. We do not care how long it takes, how hard it is, or how much we are being paid to do what we do. It is about our clients and their survival. We are all in, totally emotionally invested, because we know we can help our clients win.

My business partners and I agreed that this was our cause, and we made it part of everything we did. We became a cause-driven business, and our company grew substantially. Yours can, too, when you find a purpose—find a cause. Put money on the back burner and live that purpose and cause for your employees. As you do, your team will buy in, and your company will experience growth and success like never before.

Just remember to be patient and stay the course you have set. Nothing happens as quickly as you would like. Stay engaged in your cause, resist the human tendency to focus solely on making an easy buck, and it will happen. Soon, money will be the least of your worries. Serving your customers will be the only mission that permeates your thoughts and consumes your tear-filled prayers on bended knee.

A cause-driven business will motivate your employees to work at their best levels—whether you are watching them or not, whether it's hard or not, and whether you pay them a lot or not. You cannot fake this. You cannot pretend. Only authentic cause-driven businesses will inspire their employees to provide *Wow!* customer experiences.

So, get on board and take the reins. Implement true principles that will allow your team to see the vision of your company. Then map out how your vision will be realized in each customer interaction.

Hank Brigman refers to those moments when your company interacts with your customer as "touchpoints"—influential actions initiated by a communication, a human contact, or a physical or sensory interaction. Collectively, touchpoints create your customers' experience.[1]

But before you can even consider each customer touchpoint, you must step up, do the hard work to answer what is important to you, and know what is true. With all the turmoil, deception, and strife surrounding us, we can find it difficult to determine what is fact and what is not. There is comfort and a sense of peace that comes when you take a step back and consider common truths we all agree on and adhere to in one way or another, and there is no bigger one than the truth about customer experience.

As you discover principles you value and develop your understanding of them, you will naturally become self-motivated to forgo old habits, including weaknesses and vices that keep you from embarking on a path to a life patterned after excellence. You will gain a quiet sense of confidence in all the choices you make, caring less about what others think of you. Contentment will be prevalent in your life, because the truths you have discovered and chosen to live by have enabled you to experience a life reserved for only a precious few.

This does not mean that the journey to discover and live that truth isn't filled with roadblocks, challenges, and setbacks. Human tendency keeps us from winning moments. Many times, we are caught unaware that we are in a moment. Other times, we may recognize that someone should do something in a moment, unaware that the "someone" is us. Even when we recognize a moment in which we know we can create meaning for others, we recoil and fail to act.

CHAPTER 3

AGENCY IN THE MOMENT

To overcome human tendency, you need to discover and coura-geously live by truth. To truly live by truth, you have to *act* on it. Agency is our right to choose the path we take as well as the life we will lead. Without making choices that align with the truth about serving others, you'll never really succeed in business. This goes way beyond what is commonly known as customer service. It's a way of life.

Sure, many people are born into advantages that others do not have, but no matter where we are born or the circumstances in which we grow up, we all can choose to improve. And no one can strip us of our freedom to choose how we respond to a situation, no matter how emotionally charged, unfair, or out of control it may be. The choice is ours, and our choices shape who we are and who we'll become in this life. This truth is sure and undeniable. We can act independently of our circumstances living by truth.

Agency empowers us to define who we are and makes us the author of our own lives. It enables us to act as opposed to being acted upon. The "prisons" we build with choices like doing drugs or viewing lewd images can also take away our agency. We are free to choose, but wrong choices will make us less free. Addiction enslaves and impedes our ability to act independently and clearly, and it may lead to literal imprisonment as well. In fact, anything we do in excess, from eating to working out, can also enslave us and deny us our agency. Too much of a bad *or* good thing can hinder our independence and the development of lasting relationships, meaningful accomplishments, and many winning moments.

To experience true freedom—true agency—we must learn to forget ourselves, doggedly do what is right, and prioritize each other as much as, if not more than, ourselves. When we lose ourselves in the service of others, we find our true selves as our fears fade into the background. A choice to live by truth creates a higher purpose that drives our actions instead of selfish ambition. At the very least, it's a great way to keep out of trouble!

So what does any of this have to do with business, creating meaningful moments for customers, and living a life patterned after excellence?

THE ZERO MOMENT OF TRUTH

Google coined the phrase *zero moment of truth* to help businesses understand how consumers buy. Forget the old three-step buying model of stimulus (traditional advertising), point of sale, and customer experience, Google argues. There is a fourth moment that's as—if not more—important, a moment that occurs between stimulus (thinking about buying) and point of sale (actually buying). This critical moment is the zero moment of truth: when consumers get to know you. They go online to read reviews, comparison shop, consider options, dig into details, and read more about whatever they are considering buying. In this moment, when customers are seeking information and learning more about your product or service, they will decide whether you are a company they want to buy from.

Whether or not you agree with Google, the zero moment of truth allows your business to stand out and lets you make a difference in the decision. Agency gives us the power to write our own stories when it comes to creating meaningful moments and experiences for our customers. But this can only happen if we *choose* to do so and learn to be more aware of what is happening around us right now.

MINDFUL AGENCY

Great customer service and creating meaningful experiences are about seizing opportunities to go above and beyond at the right time. This is extremely difficult if you are not present in the moment. You have to be consciously engaged in what customers are saying as well as in their tone and intent. You must have genuine concern for their well-being. We miss more moments than we think because we are so preoccupied with our self-interests or are so stuck in the past or worrying about the future that we miss what's really going on in front of us.

However, if we are constantly aware of our customers' (and our own) values and remain in constant contact with the truth, all we have to do is act. When the moment presents itself, we must *make decisions based on what is right and true*, rather than on selfishness and fleeting circumstances. *This* is where we can shine as the hero of our story.

While my company was still in its initial growth phase, I was running a booth at an event in downtown Philadelphia with one of my partners. We were spending virtually every penny we had on the travel and expenses for the event. But this was not unusual for us. Big risk-taking was commonplace for me back then. We were trying to do whatever was necessary to make my customer service training idea work. I didn't know how long it would take; I just knew that if I kept at it, it would work.

While at the booth, I was doing everything I could to pull in prospects walking by, but my partner, Barry, had disappeared. Traffic at the booth was slow. We needed everything we had, but while I was there hustling, he was nowhere to be found.

I was getting angry. Here I was, working my tail off, while he was—what?—just hanging out somewhere? Meandering around the event?

Finally, I saw him making his way back to the booth with some other guy I did not recognize. As he walked up to me, he could tell something was wrong by the look on my face. He hesitantly introduced the guy. Then he introduced him again, with special emphasis on who the guy was.

That second introduction snapped me out of my heated stupor. This guy my partner had walked up with was the vice president of customer relations at a major manufacturer in our industry.

I pushed the angered look on my face into a forced smile while my partner quickly smoothed over my failed first impression, explaining to the VP that I had just moved boxes to the booth and was still getting over some back pain. We all chuckled as Barry explained that he had been trying to convince me to take some pain meds and rest my feet. I reached for my back with one of my hands for effect during Barry's attempt to save the moment and let out a humming groan to help sell the story.

It must have worked, because the three of us soon left the booth, where nothing was happening, and sat on a nearby couch to talk shop. We've been doing business with the manufacturer ever since.

My partner could have taken offense at my state of mind when he approached me with a golden prospect. He could have been distracted with the angered look on my face, as I had gotten distracted by assuming the worst of him. Instead, he did not let me keep us from winning that moment, and he helped me prevent it too.

Life is full of moments of opportunity like this. If you want to win them, you need to learn to recognize when you're in one. But how do you do that? The Pattern for Excellence provides a framework for getting past ourselves in order to recognize and act on pivotal moments.

I've listed the eight principles of the Pattern for Excellence below. Each of these principles is blocked by certain human tendencies, which we'll discuss throughout the rest of the book.

Be Positive

Moments are often missed because we are so bogged down in selfish tasks and our own agendas that we're not present in those moments. It's even worse when we're embroiled in negative thoughts. Not only can we miss an opportunity by being too focused—too locked in our own heads—on all the possible negative outcomes of an event, but we can drive people away because of a poor attitude—creating those negative outcomes ourselves.

Your opportunity to shine and experience meaningful moments comes in the service of another. Only when your attitude is positive and your mind free of the past or an imagined future can you proceed with a heightened social awareness in the present. When that happens, everything that is going on in front of you in the present begins to slow down. All your senses are subconsciously engaged in the moment in front of you and the role you can play to create a meaningful experience for someone else.

Be Confident

The thing that separates players from fans is work. Professionals sharpen their skill sets and put in countless hours of work long before a game is played. If you are not well practiced and prepared to act in a moment, you may not see that it was yours for the taking until after the fact.

Your attitude may allow you to recognize the opportunity for *someone* to serve another. However, you may not realize in that pivotal moment that the someone could have been *you*. Therein lies the difference: Fans consider what someone can do in a moment, whereas players have developed the mechanics and muscle memory to *act* in that moment, without having to think.

The difference is best characterized as a contest between ego and confidence. Our ego allows us to perceive the world in a way that is out of balance with reality. For example, we might think we would have known what to do in a situation, but there's no substance to that knowledge, and certainly no agency. Confidence, on the other hand, is based on truth, and it leads to—and comes from—agency. When the moment arrives, confident players *play* while the rest watch in awe or even envy. Which are you in your profession—a player or a fan?

Listen

Part of becoming present is to listen and retain what is happening in the moment. If you can emotionally connect with another person in the moment by listening first—and remaining present to their expression, tone, and intent—your capacity for winning moments will be greatly enhanced.

Care

As the saying goes, no one cares about how much you know until he or she knows how much you care. We can only become present and connect with another when we show genuine empathy and respect for his or her worth in pivotal moments.

Give

We can be such selfish and entitled creatures—always looking out for number one. This is why it is often easier to receive or even take than to give. By giving first, we create meaningful experiences and begin to win moments and build long-term relationships.

Ask

Meaningful experiences do not often just fall in your lap. You must learn to be accountable to the moment by asking yourself what is missing in any given situation. Once you have uncovered what is needed and considered what is the right response, respond accordingly. Fear can often get in the way, especially when you consider the risk involved in the moment you want to affect. However, to win the moment, you must courageously take action, and that means asking—for help, for clarity—while in the pursuit of a business opportunity.

Build Value

We should endeavor to consciously create value for others. Now don't get me wrong here: All things must be done in order. Sometimes, when we want to create value in a moment, our ambition can get the better of our judgment. We have a responsibility, a role we play. We should learn to create value within that responsibility. As you do well with and multiply what you have within your responsibility, your boss, if he or she is smart, will give you more freedom and responsibilities. The two often go hand in hand.

Be Grateful

Life gives us a body and a right to choose how to respond. Because we are here with air in our lungs and have freedom to choose, we deserve nothing. For this reason alone, should we not do as much good as possible with the time we have? Should we not choose to live with gratitude in our hearts for as long as there is breath in our lungs or for as long as our freedom will allow? A grateful heart helps keep those moments we win in perspective.

These truths are easier said and understood than they are consistently done. If it were not so, I would be out of business. Think about it: There would be no need to hold thousands of trainees accountable in our coaching program if they were already doing what we teach. Why? To *know* is not enough; *you must do.*

★

RISE AND WIN THE MOMENT

Getting out of bed to hit the gym at the crack of dawn is hard. It's much easier to push the snooze button. Learning to rise and be present at the imperative time is how moments are won. You can't win in the metaphorical game of life if you don't rise to take the shot. This is why we must learn to discipline ourselves to recognize moments and rise to them instead of shrinking—whether we win or lose.

Rising in moments is a reflex that we all need. Being proactive instead of recoiling on initial impulse makes you an agent that acts as opposed to an object that is acted upon. This powerful state of mind breeds success in extraordinary living. It's how leaders are born and meaningful work gets done. By now, you are beginning to see that the only thing that keeps you from being the person you were meant to be is, well, you. You are your own worst enemy. You are your biggest critic. You keep yourself from winning moments.

To rise, you must develop the ability to recognize and act on moments as they occur. This can be done in three easy steps. First, you must choose to live in the now by focusing your mind on the present moment happening right now in front of you. Second, human emotion can keep you from doing as you ought, which is why you must learn to do right independently of how you feel. Just learn to cognitively push aside any human emotion or natural tendency that may make you shrink while in a moment. Third, learn to courageously act on first impulse in accordance with the truth you know.

The pursuit of truth needs to be akin to the pursuit of oxygen to us. We must want to see, hear, and understand truth as much as we want air while underwater.

★

OWN THE MOMENT OR GET COOKED IN THE SQUAT

In early 2017, refugees from the Congo arrived in Salt Lake City. A longtime friend asked me to help him move donated furniture into the refugees' apartments so they would have a place to sit as well as beds to sleep on. For whatever reason, I declined. That day, my friend and his children experienced some amazing connections and positive emotions because they performed this act of service. The way they looked at life changed for the better. They gained a perspective my kids and I could have shared had I accepted his offer and helped.

Only when I saw the pictures of my friend's service opportunity did I realize what I had missed. The moment was gone. I had missed it because I was caught up in myself and how going to help out would be time consuming and inconvenient. I had failed to consider how the experience would positively affect my children and me.

Zig Ziglar calls this "getting cooked in the squat." Maybe you have to be from the South to get this, but biscuits and gravy are a big deal there. Whether the biscuit dough rises or not, it is still getting cooked. When biscuits rise, they are soft in the middle and tasty. But when they're cooked in the squat, they come out of the oven no bigger than silver dollars. They are hard and often thrown out.

The lesson I learned from that missed opportunity: When in a moment of truth, don't shrink; rise.

Because we have a right to our own response, we are agents who can act independently of what is going on around us. However, acting to create meaningful moments can sometimes feel inconvenient. We can get caught feeling too tired, preoccupied, or like we just have no desire to do the work. But when you know the right course of action to take while in a moment, how you feel in that moment is irrelevant.

To act on truth that is independent of how you feel is heroic. It takes practice and discipline to overcome what some may deem as "normal" but is, in fact, a self-defeating human tendency. Acting on truth, independent of circumstance or events, is how moments are won and lives are fulfilled, for you and those you serve. In effect, you are edified together. Failing to do so makes us subject to our circumstances or events as they occur. Without realizing, we allow those events or circumstances to influence our decisions, instead of letting what is right influence *them*. We shrink instead of acting in the moment, because our hearts fail us. We are no longer agents that act in accordance with the truth. Instead, we cower to emotionally charged human tendencies that would have us behave in a way inconsistent with our ideals. As opposed to living a life with many joyful moments won, we selfishly live by sensations; we forgo our agency for a temporary fix to mute an inner emptiness that only purposeful living can fill.

Moments are fleeting. If you do not act immediately, they will pass you by, and the opportunity to win them will be gone. You will have given up your right to improve while you are here on this earth and thus make you and it better—to use your agency to write the best version of your life's story. The power is in you to act in moments without detours or delays.

Human emotion or tendencies can enslave our better judgment in moments. Rather than missing moments of truth, learn to discipline yourself—to ignore your body's emotional responses. Learn to act, not react. Avoid the allure of temporary sensations that sap your freedom to independently act. While in a moment, stay collected, rational, and focused on what you know you should do. Learn to live in the now and courageously act on truth. Just remember: Mere knowledge is not enough. We must learn to embody the truth we know, to act on it. It is about doing and becoming as opposed to merely knowing. If it were easy, everyone would do it, but this is what it takes to become the best you—the you that you were born to be.

CHAPTER 4

FREEDOM FROM NEGATIVITY

I n fourth grade I was called "hyperactive," and that became who I was: Hyperactive Brigham. There was certainly a lot of evidence to support that title, and one look at my family pictures during that time is all you need to know how much they believed that's who I was: my dad's hands in every shot, white-knuckle tight around my biceps. He said it was the only way to get me to hold still because I was always on the go. My parents were constantly at work to keep me from getting hurt or accidentally hurting someone else. My mother described me as living on the edge, without fear (my pain tolerance was high). My aunt predicted that I would not make it past the age of sixteen.

I did, of course, and when I was twenty-two, I took an ADHD test that measures hyperactivity. The test results showed that my hyperactivity had miraculously disappeared. That's when I first realized that the stories of my hyperactivity were exactly that: stories. For better or worse, stories like that have power over us, and perhaps none are more damaging than the stories that others tell about us—and that become the stories we let define who we are. Sure, these stories can build us up, but more often, they become impediments to our progress for as long as we believe them.

Everyone has challenges or difficulties to overcome. But it's up to you which stories you let define you. Believe no one who makes it a point to remind you of your shortcomings or disabilities—even yourself. Refuse to believe that is the end of your story. We all must face our fears and begin to discover, courageously live by and explore, what is real about who we are and what we are capable of.

You can write your own story of positivity and success. Simply put, stories only have bearing on our lives if we let them. *Instead of believing the stories that are told about you, let them motivate you to improve.* Seize opportunities to become a version of yourself that embraces the truth, focused on your strengths, talents, and potential rather than on why you can't reach your goals.

By the time I took that ADHD test, I had long exceeded my aunt's expectations. I understood that my story had not been written yet and that what I was going to be was on me. Was I a hyper kid? Yes! Did that bring me down? No! It was not a setback at all once I learned to harness my energy positively with intense focus. I know I can be easily distracted at times, but when it counts, I can become extremely engaged too. Everything else going on around me falls into the background when I am engaged in what I deem important. This intense focus has helped me win more moments than I can count. In fact, I actually *hope* that someone says I can't do what I want to do. I feed off that doubt. I let it push me to go beyond what others—and even I—might initially think is possible.

To do this, you just need to believe in yourself and write bigger stories. Limits are only limiting until you reach them and figure out a way past them. It's our lack of optimism that keeps us from living in an extraordinary way.

BELIEVE IN YOURSELF

History is full of people who did not let the stories others told about them affect their belief in who they could become and what they would accomplish. They made possible what others saw as impossible. Only when we succumb to the stories told about us and believe them as our true identities are we kept from winning moments. *Let others be complacent or make excuses while you win moments and opportunities they never knew existed.*

When you do this, you'll begin to see that opportunity is all around you—opportunities you never saw before. When you fail to believe in yourself, you succumb to a human tendency that pulls you toward particular behaviors, thought processes, or actions, and leads you away from opportunity. In other words, without careful consideration, the tug and pull of our human tendencies can, contrary to our better judgment, make us shrink.

By shrinking in a moment, we create that internal prison that negates our ability to discover and live by truth. Choosing to act well in moments increases the flow of opportunity, whereas caving to natural tendency impedes the flow of opportunity. There is no shortage of opportunity, just a diminished capacity to recognize that opportunity. Remember, you do not know your limits until you experience them. And you don't know how you can surpass those limits until you try (and fail and try again). When in a moment, don't shrink. Seize it!

We all are guilty of shrugging our shoulders as we make the wrong choice. Whether everyone is doing it is irrelevant. Even when we think to do something nice for someone else while in a moment, we push the thought aside for one reason or another. Although we should know better than to suppress a generous thought, our actions are often inconsistent with what we know is right. Why? Because our goodwill may go unnoticed or judged as over the top or unnecessary. In all such cases and more, you cannot change the fact that you *knew* better and yet chose not to *do* better.

To begin asserting our agency—writing our own story—we must learn to recognize and rise in moments instead of caving to tendency. A true principle cannot remain in the human mind at the same time as its opposing human tendency. In an imperative moment, the true principle or its opposing human tendency will prevail, with lasting consequences on the person we become. Inevitably, what we become depends on how we choose to act in moments. In this case, we can choose to be and act positively (the first principle of the Pattern for Excellence) and overcome our tendency toward negativity.

For example, as I wrote this book, it had been a decade since I found myself on the verge of bankruptcy. My brother Ben had written me a letter during that difficult time, sharing a story that greatly impacted me. He had just moved on from one of the most rewarding jobs he had ever had, with the US Border Patrol, and he told me the story of how he overcame the trials of the Border Patrol Academy, one of the hardest things he had ever gone through in his life. The physical training sounded brutal, with an instructor that pushed Ben and his cohort as hard as any boot camp you've ever seen in the movies. But that wasn't the only challenge for my brother: He had to learn Spanish, too, and in some ways he made that harder than the physical training:

> *I failed the first three Spanish tests. One was an easy vocabulary test, with really basic words. A voice recording would say the word in Spanish, and I had to choose the English word of what I heard. Yes, I failed it. I couldn't hear the language. The instructor told me that he had never seen anyone fail all three of the first tests and pass the course . . .*
>
> *I continued to study. It was hard for me to see some people picking it up like it was nothing and me studying like mad. When others actually took the weekends off, I was working very hard. I did very little other than study. I was on my knees pleading for help. I was under a great deal of*

pressure for several months. What would I do if I were fired? I trudged along and studied so hard.

My brother passed the Spanish tests, and he withstood physical training too. Then, in the letter, he reminded me why he was telling me all this: "With this story," he wrote, "I hope to have illustrated that after some of the toughest periods of my life have come the greatest rewards."

This letter from my big brother, which was open and honest about a difficult time in his life and the struggles he faced, was the best thing for me to hear. It got me out of the self-loathing "I can't do this" pity party going on inside my head back then.

Perhaps the biggest lie in human history is when we tell ourselves we can't do it. The truth is we *WON'T* do it because we are currently *CHOOSING* to not pay the price that it will take to *DO* it. The question was not whether Ben was capable of learning Spanish. It was whether he was willing to do what was necessary for HIM to learn Spanish—even if that meant that he would have to work harder than any of his peers. Stop the lies! Decide that you can. Currently, you won't . . . Why? Because until now, you have not been willing to come to grips with the truth. And the truth is that you have no idea how capable you are because you simply have not pushed yourself that hard.

Agency gives us a right to choose. We have a choice. Ben's letter reminded me that I could choose my response and overcome my adversity—to believe in myself and overcome pessimism.

WRITING A POSITIVE STORY

The human tendency to embrace the negative is like a virus. It spreads from person to person not through your blood or the air, but through stories. What other people say about us—and what we say about our-selves—can infect us with pessimism.

This virus makes us feel tired and melancholy instantly, and it can derail crucial moments along the way. While it's true that this conta-gion may not be as deadly as Ebola, it could kill your dreams and at the very least ruin your day and the days of everyone around you. It chokes creative thought and activity. It exhausts your energy and brings productivity to a halt. Because pessimists tend to see the worst and believe the worst will happen, a pessimistic outlook practically guar-antees individual human failure. Even when the sun shines through the rain clouds, pessimists immediately begin to talk about how it's too bright or predict when it will rain again. Why not just enjoy the sun while you have it? It's not about the weather anyway. Rather, it's about learning how to exercise your agency: the ability to act independently of circumstance.

Those who are infected with pessimism are also often carriers of other symptoms like cynicism, the inclination to believe that peo-ple are motivated purely by self-interest, and skepticism, which is an individual doubt about the truth of something, such as that certain knowledge in and of itself is impossible. Despair is also related and is a complete loss or absence of hope. Scarcity, too, can be counted as a distant relative of pessimism, as it is the state of being in short supply. All of these and more fall under the great epidemic tendency known as pessimism.

There are times I have to fight against welcoming this virus as a friend and allowing myself to wallow in self-pity or pride while I shrink from a challenge instead of figuring a way out. But I knew my big brother was right in that letter: After some of the toughest peri-ods of life often come the greatest rewards. Maybe grit is in my fam-ily's DNA. Maybe my family, all of us, are just too dumb to quit. But we know how to win moments. My big brother reminded me of that as well as the power we all have to act on principle, independently of circumstance.

Yes, I recognize that there are some circumstances we do not choose. My youngest son, Hagen, has autism. None of us chose that, but I can choose my response to his condition. I am responsible for fighting the tendency to slip into despair and negativity, to question why this happened to my son and our family. Only I can keep the pessimism, cynicism, and despair at bay within and, instead, choose love.

That's how we keep from getting the virus of negativity in business or in life. Kill the virus if you contract it: Refuse to play the blame game. Instead, choose to act on principle, and write a positive story by searching out moments you can generously affect.

PEOPLE ARE NOT TOASTERS

Picture a brand-new toaster. It is the best tool for making toast, but it doesn't do much else, and it certainly can't choose to do something different. Because it is new, it works great for making toast. But what if I take it outside and dropkick it around my street a couple of times? Would you expect it to continue to work like it did before? Probably not. A toaster is an object designed to be used by humans to perform a single act or related acts. It cannot independently act, and it can't recover from adversity.

Humans are not toasters. We can act independently, and when life kicks us around, we can perform at the same level or even better—provided we choose to remain positive. Unlike a toaster, we can learn from our mistakes—and even other people's mistakes—to improve how we do everything, including making toast. Unfortunately, choosing to use adversity to improve is the path less taken.

Many of us mistakenly believe that our bad actions are an effect of the bad things that have happened to us or the fault of someone else.

This "cause and effect" mind-set shifts responsibility away from ourselves (the only thing we can control) to objects or other people (things you cannot control). We must learn to do what most people do not: choose to win moments by recognizing that we control our responses to outside forces, and then respond with fortitude and perseverance—not blame others for our circumstances.

Pointing the finger of blame except while looking straight into a mirror shifts responsibility elsewhere and makes you an object that is acted upon, not an independent actor. For you to be extraordinary, you have to be independent and see opportunity to act independently. Each time you choose to act on principle, you become more free. Each time you shrink to human tendency, you become less free.

Shifting blame outward keeps you from making responsible inward changes. Even if it is not your fault when something goes wrong, consider what you would do if it were. What can you do—not think or say or blame, but actually do—differently to keep such a thing from happening again? With this mind-set, trial and adversity can serve as experience that contributes to your ultimate good.

TAKE CONTROL OF WHAT YOU CAN DO AND DO IT!

Twenty years ago, I accepted a job offer from Royal Hawkley to manage his marketing channels, evaluate ways to improve the customer experience, and help answer phones for his company. It was an exciting opportunity, because I was still getting my degree in marketing, and already I was being offered a job. In my mind, it couldn't get any better.

It was easy to look up to Royal and adhere to his leadership style. He commanded respect and loyalty. He surrounded himself with the right talent. He knew his strengths for sure but was also able to pull together a team to fill the voids where he was weak. He listened, cared for our well-being, and followed through on his promises. He was incredibly driven and competitive but in a quiet sort of way—no foul language or speaking ill of anyone. He also didn't brag about his successes, despite his accomplishments. Simply put, he was a true leader—the kind you would follow into battle.

One of Royal's biggest competitors back then ran a company in a small town adjacent to our market. He ran very smart and strategic marketing campaigns that, as evidence of his obvious genius, were extremely similar to the ones we had run in the previous weeks in our own market. Each time I discovered one of these sincerest-form-of-flattery campaigns, I would rush into Royal's office, up in arms about our competitor's audacious behavior. Royal would attentively listen but never seemed worried.

It felt like a middle school test, with our competitor trying to look over our company's shoulder to see the answers. As I tried to figure out the business equivalent of hunching over the desk and wrapping my arm around my test, Royal told me to just worry about my own work.

Then one day, our competitor came out with a brilliant campaign I had never seen before. The advertisement began with how the company's building had burned to the ground in a tragic accident. The ad featured a very convincing picture of an ash heap that had once been a building in a field. The text explained how the business owner's tragic loss was the customer's gain. He was low on cash and in a fix. He stored several home heating and cooling systems in an adjacent warehouse for the upcoming busy season. Instead of waiting until the summer, homeowners who bought one of those systems now would get it at almost wholesale—a savings of $1,000 or more.

It was pure genius. It was so well articulated that by the time I was done reading it, I wanted to buy his product myself.

I ran into Royal's office and said, "We need to set our building on fire!"

He listened to my concern with his usual patience, but when I had finished speaking, his response was different from the norm. He leaned in across the desk, looked at me eyeball to eyeball, and said, "Brigham, I'm not concerned with what he is doing. In fact, I don't really care what any of our competitors are doing. What I care about is what *we* are doing. You have a job to do. Time to create. Go and do it."

Royal was right. What our competitor was doing had nothing to do with us or what we were doing. It didn't matter if they copied us or outdid us; we had to outdo ourselves. I could not control the elements. I could not control other people. I could, however, control myself. I had a job to do. I could choose to hunker down and go to work on what I could control.

We face these choices in business and in life every day at all points in our lives. For example, during one Fourth of July parade, my young nephew sat crying on the street curb because he did not get any of the candy being thrown from the floats. As the other kids scrambled for candy with each float that came by, he sat there crying.

Whose fault is it that he was not getting any candy? You could say that the passersby on the floats were not being fair. You could blame the other kids because they were not sharing with my nephew. But you should start by saying it was my nephew's fault, because he stopped working for the candy and instead shrank from the challenge and cried.

Whether it's harsh or not is irrelevant. My nephew could not control the people on the floats or the actions of his cousins and the other kids near him on the street. He could, however, control himself. Just like all of us, he could choose to act and go after what he wanted.

There is one more thought to consider on this point: What if my nephew had some sort of physical or emotional impediment that kept him from going after the candy that was thrown out to him? Would he then have enough of an excuse for his inaction?

It would certainly make it harder but not impossible. When my son Hagen, who is autistic, really wants something like candy, a toy, or to dash away from his parents, he usually finds a way to get what he wants. He does not let autism stop him. Why would you let a disability—perceived or real—stop you?

To shrink or to act is a choice we make. No matter how hard that choice, we still get to choose our response. Choose optimism. You'll live happier, and studies show that you'll live longer too.

Optimism counteracts the effects of pessimism. An abundance mentality stands opposite to scarcity and helps you look upon all that you have with contentment or a state of happiness and satisfaction with the good in your life. Hope drowns out despair and is a feeling of expectation or a desire for a good thing to happen. Hope helps us walk with faith in ourselves and others, even when the odds are clearly against us. No matter how bad it gets, things often have a way of working themselves out. Choose to always believe in and hope for the best possible outcome—and then work toward it to make it happen. By doing so, you, too, are an optimist. This abundance mentality will benefit you greatly when you realize all that you have—rather than focus on what you do not—in everything you do.

Kim S. Cameron, professor of management at the University of Michigan, teaches optimism, the concept of positive leadership, and its heliotropic effect. Some of the outcomes from his studies on optimism refer to the tendency in all living systems toward positive energy and away from negative energy. From single-cell organisms to complex ecosystems, everything alive has an inherent inclination toward the positive and away from the negative.

He also teaches that there are three critical components for a workplace culture: compassion, forgiveness, and gratitude.[1] Reworded, we get love, patience, and kindness. These positive components can be just as contagious as rudeness and crudeness. It may take more work, but the result will speak for itself with many moments won.

Simply put, we can respond to personal or social irritations with smiles instead of a scowl or by giving warm praise instead of icy indifference. Optimism is a choice. Choosing to be happy, independently of the events and circumstances around us, is at times easier said than done. You may not be able to immediately transition your emotional state from negative to positive like turning on a light switch, but you can work at it, and when we project love, understanding, and compassion as our first response, others are more inclined to respond in a like manner.

FILL YOUR DEAD SPACE WITH OPTIMISM

What we put out in the world is often what we get back, and what we put out in our "dead space" says a lot about that. Dead space—unstructured time—is a killer of productivity and inner growth. You can develop optimistic muscles with daily habits that exercise those muscles to fend off events and circumstances as they occur. There is a lot of dead space in our days. You control what you listen to, watch, and read during that time. You can fill it with positivity if you so choose. Technology has made it easier than ever before to control the story going on in your head at any given moment. "Stinking thinking" happens to everyone during dead space. But you can choose positivity in the way you choose to spend that time.

India-born centenarian Tao Porchon-Lynch, the world's oldest yoga teacher (according to the Guinness World Records), gives this mantra as her secret to longevity: "Nothing is impossible." After a career that included fighting for the French Resistance, as well as being a model, actress, and activist, she's taught yoga for over forty-five years, despite having three hip replacement operations. She lives in Hartsdale, New York, where she still teaches popular yoga classes. She has four secrets to living a long and productive life:

★ Be an optimist: "Whatever you put in your mind materializes."

★ Be courageous: "Don't spend time on 'I can't.'"

★ Focus on breathing: "Everything has energy; it's the breath of life."

★ Dress in heels: "I wear high-heeled shoes so that I'm completely energizing my instep all the time."

OK, I do not plan on wearing high heels anytime soon, but I sure like her style.

Yoga is awesome for daily positive reinforcement, and it's a great way to rejuvenate your body. Tao is over a hundred now and started doing yoga at a very young age. When she was eight, she saw a group of boys performing crazy postures on a beach in India. Her aunt told her that because she was a girl, yoga was not for her. But Tao wanted to do it, and she said, "If boys can do it, so can I."[2]

★

CLIMB OUT OF THE CRAB BUCKET

The nicest neighbors, friends, and even family members can diminish the achievements or successes of individuals around them. Sometimes this is unconscious and without malice, but other times this stems from envy, conspiracy, jealousy, spite, or other emotions rooted in selfishness. One way or another, we all sometimes halt each other's progress, especially if someone seems to be achieving at a much faster pace than the rest of the group.

This is called the *crab bucket mentality,* a common social epidemic that means if the rest of us cannot have it, neither can you.

Picture a bucket of crabs. As one courageous crab begins to pull its way out of the dirty old bucket, his fellow crabs pull him back

continued

---

down into the bucket. Individually, any of the crabs could escape their impending demise; instead, they grab at each other, preventing any from escaping.

Our social circles should build and reward our optimism—lift us up and support us, not pull us back down into the bucket. Family and friends should cheer us on as we move into the unknown and even the undone.

If only this were common. As we dream something that is hard, if not impossible, and endeavor to make that dream a reality, we often face negativity and worse from those closest to us as they unwittingly endeavor to pull us back down into the bucket.

But even worse is when we pull ourselves down. Our lack of self-belief can be a vicious enemy. It is a lie. To be human is often to be one's greatest critic—your own worst enemy instead of the hero of your story. Succumbing to negativity keeps us from being our best selves, the heroes, and makes us as untrue to ourselves as our peers can be toward us. Don't stop believing. Be positive and true to your conscience. If the work you are doing is something you know will succeed as long as you keep at it, never quit. Never quit. Ever!

★

DON'T LIMIT YOURSELF!

As long as we breathe, we will continue to face difficult and challenging times, and with each breath we can find the strength to choose the light to combat the dark. Remember always that as humans, our abilities are limitless; we simply do not know the full scope of our potential until we reach for it. Do not permit yourself, or anyone else for that matter, to keep you from seeking, finding, and accepting the truth for what it is. And the truth is that you do not know what you are capable of doing.

Practice self-awareness so you can recognize when others are limiting you, holding you back, or pulling you down emotionally. Learn to overcome selfish behavior that keeps you and others down. Learn to cheer on yourself and others to edify each other and strengthen existing relationships. Celebrate each other's achievements. You all deserve it. Limit your attention to the news, and instead listen to books, uplifting music, and educational podcasts. Most importantly, when you seek out and discover truth, live it. Experience it. Let no one and nothing stop you from doing what you know in your heart is right.

Self-doubt and lack of social support are among the biggest things that keep us from bettering ourselves and the world we live in. Imagine the good we could do within ourselves, within our homes, and for the world if we just believed in and supported each other. We must simply make the choice to let go of limiting beliefs—those self-imposed prisons that keep us from living in extraordinary ways. We must learn to break free from them and embrace more enlightened ones. This is not easy; if it were, everyone would do it.

Breaking free is key to overcoming our tendencies and winning moments. Search out the truth. Consider what can be and start believing that you can. Believe that all things are possible for yourself and others. Believing is seeing; you must learn to simply let your mind wrap around new and innovative ideas instead of letting social norms dictate your actions. Believe that you can and doggedly go after it. As you do, you'll win moments that will change the world.

CHAPTER 5

FREEDOM FROM EGO

After I'd figured out that I needed to follow my own advice, my company was taking off like a rocket. We had carved a niche in the industry with our call-handling coaching program. We had strong relationships with our clients and were in negotiations with a larger training company in our industry that did not offer the type of ongoing coaching we provided. Their clients were already signing up with us to provide accountability and results to their call-handling teams. As this larger training company began to seriously consider the idea of a partnership with us, I got excited about the possibilities. Each conference call we had together seemed to bring us closer to a deal. Until it didn't. They decided not to work with us and instead would offer something similar to our services in-house.

To say the least, I was displeased. I reacted with disappointment and incredulity. I remember asking myself, *How in the world do they believe that they are better off not working with us? Can't they see why many of their clients have signed up to experience the kind of one-on-one accountability coaching we offer?*

So, I decided to do something about it. I took my top salesperson and flew to Nashville to attend—uninvited—one of the larger company's biannual client events. To make this really bad idea worse, I brought several bright hunter orange shirts with our logo on the front and handed them out to our clients who were there. Many wore them the next day.

My top salesperson and I felt the stunt was a huge success, but I'm sure you can already guess that it wasn't. The training company that had decided against a partnership with us was, shall we say, unimpressed, and I squandered any chance of a working relationship with this potentially valuable partner in the future. Yes, the prospective partner had said no. But so what? *No*, in and of itself, has a short shelf life. I needed to think in longer time frames. And I needed to grow up. A *no* today does not mean a *no* tomorrow if you can keep your ego in check—rather than react out of self-interest—and leave the door open to future discussions. Instead, when this door of opportunity momentarily shut, I sealed the seams.

Obviously, my ill-advised stunt was motivated by my bruised ego. I let it and the emotions that it filled me with get the best of me, and I lost all perspective for one "gotcha" moment. Today, that training company I offended still declines to discuss partnering with us. Would things have turned out differently had I not let my ego get the best of me? My company is much more established now. It would benefit both companies to have some sort of collaborative relationship. If only I had swallowed my ego back then, thanked them for their consideration, and continued to build and grow my company in our industry. They would have, at the very least, been able to see our continued growth and success from an untainted viewpoint. But because of my behavior, driven by ego, we'll likely never know what could have been.

CONFIDENCE VERSUS EGO

Ego is your sense of self-esteem or self-importance—that part of your mind that mediates between the conscious and the unconscious. When ego is held in check, it can create a subconscious picture that depicts what's real about you as well as those with whom you interact.

However, when your ego is left unchecked, whether in failure or success, it can turn into a human tendency that makes you lose perspective, leading to self-deception and self-sabotage. Your ego can and will negatively affect your judgment and keep you from learning.

Ego is *not* the same as confidence. Being and remaining self-assured in one's ability—in success and failure—is what we call confidence. If you have the mechanics of what you do down cold because you have put in the work, it is easy to believe in yourself and have faith in your capacity to perform at a high level, no matter the result. This belief in ourselves and our personal strengths, attributes, and work is vital to our success. As you carry yourself with confidence, it becomes easy for others to believe in you as well. But just because you've had a few successes doesn't mean that you have arrived with nothing more to learn.

Continual learning, hard work, and success are what brought you to that state of self-assurance. But if you're not careful, confidence can morph into ego, creating false perceptions of yourself. Simply put, there's a fine line between being confident and becoming egotistical.

THE WARNING SIGNS OF
CONFIDENCE BECOMING EGO

Do you need to be right?

Confident people can readily admit that they do not have all of the answers and are open to different points of view; egotistical people tend to argue their points of view, certain that everyone else is wrong and that they are right.

Do you seek validation, accolades, and approval at all costs?

Confident people feel no need to brag about themselves or their successes; egotistical people incessantly brag about themselves and how great they are, reciting all of their successes over and over again.

continued

Do you ask for feedback—and attentively listen to that feedback?

Confident people are usually good listeners, making them inviting and approachable even if they carry themselves with swagger and are in positions of power; egotistical people only want to hear how great they are and thus tend to turn others off with their bravado.

Do you make fun of others but refuse to laugh at yourself?

Confident people are not afraid to be themselves or have fun and make light of themselves from time to time; egotistical people never lighten up and act as if they are above the idea of having fun.

Do you collaborate well with others or see them as a means to an end?

Confident people don't want to, need to, or think they can do it all themselves. They readily work with others to achieve common goals. Egotistical people see most jobs and people as beneath them and those above them as people to be beaten in order for them to win.

Are you still learning?

Applied learning and working well with others develops your confidence; egotistical people have stopped learning and see learning as a threat to their being right.

So how do you develop your confidence and at the same time keep your ego in check? Just continue doing the very things that made you self-assured in the first place. Most of all, keep learning. Keep your mind open to new ideas. Keep questioning yourself. Learn to work well with others to accomplish amazing things. Accept the fact that your successes make you no better than anyone else.

Try to remember what creates confidence—success derived from open-mindedness, applied learning, and an uncanny ability to work well with others. If I had done that, I would never have listened to my ego and gone to Nashville with those orange shirts.

★

THE STAGES OF LEARNING

Kids often get stuck in absolutes when they say things like "I can't do it" or "I don't know how." Adults do it too. We begin working on something new and quickly decide that we cannot do it and that we'll never be able to do it. As a result, we quit. But as long as you keep pushing forward with your learning—as long as you maintain your commitment and the time you put into it—ego will never completely stunt your continued growth and progress. You might make mistakes or experience setbacks, but as long as those mistakes do not create a tendency to question your capacity to continue learning, you will stay in a growth state. Only when we set up mental blocks and entertain absolutes instead of exploring opportunity and possibility do we stop growing.

Instead of setting up barriers that impede learning, accept that growing pains along the way are part of the learning process. And if you transcend the pain, you reach the ultimate stage in Noel Butch's Four Stages of Competence for learning any skill:[1]

* Unconscious Incompetence

* Conscious Incompetence

* Conscious Competence

* Unconscious Competence

Unconscious Incompetence

In this stage, ignorance is bliss. You don't know what you don't know. All things are still possible. This is your unconscious state of mind before any learning begins. You believe you can do things like play an instrument, excel at a sport, or lose that weight without ever having tried. This is a great mind-set to have, but thinking is not doing, and those who get stuck here are completely unaware of the difference or afraid to try because they will be exposed as incompetent. You might think you can do it, but you cannot because you have not paid the price. You are a fan, not a player.

Conscious Incompetence

This is an exciting time but painful, especially for those with big egos. It's where talking stops and learning through focused action—and thus the emotional and physical pain that comes with that learning—begins. You realize you don't play anything that sounds like music when you pick up that instrument. You suck at the sport you are playing. And losing weight (at least in the long term) is not as easy as cutting calories or taking a walk around the block. You become conscious of your incompetence and understand that you will have to push on through the pain. Continued hard work is the only way to benefit from what you are learning if you want to get better and achieve your end goal. At this stage, the learning curve quickly becomes mammoth. You'll feel weak and inadequate. The physical and emotional pain will continue as you fail again and again. You will struggle not to hate the fact that there is always something holding you back or that there is always someone better than you. Excuses can start creeping in and impede your progress. You may lose focus or grow tired of being continuously humbled. However, if you don't fight through it, you will quit and never fully realize your life's destiny.

Conscious Competence

If you are able to endure the hardship that comes with phase two, you will at one point or another find yourself building internal momentum as you finally begin to experience tangible progress in your learning. In this stage relief comes, as a measure of self-confidence begins to sprout from the small successes that result from your hard work and intense focus. At this point, you know that if you keep applying yourself, you can do it. You know because you have finally begun to experience progress in your efforts. The evidence is found in the positive outcome of your continued practice. You can play that song. You finally begin to excel on the field and beat your opponent. You kept the weight off long after bathing suit season! Although you're still somewhat uncomfortable, as long as you stay engaged and focused, you will experience success and hunger for more.

Unconscious Competence

You continue to apply yourself for hours and hours, always open to what you don't yet know and confident in what you do know. You experience fewer and fewer pitfalls and more progress and success. This is how you arrive at the ultimate stage: Here, you have mastered what you do and are able to perform automatically without having to think about what it is you are doing. Your performance is now built into your muscle memory, and you have become so adept at your trade that you do it naturally. This transformation is absolutely miraculous when you consider where you were at the start of your learning curve. Yet, when you consider the work and practice you have put into it, the result becomes rudimentary.

You can apply the Four Stages of Competence to anything you are learning in business and in life. It will help you push on, keep your ego in check, and remember what it takes to be a player, not just a fan.

Overcoming Obstacles

I have and continue to experience these stages with every obstacle I face, but none is more physically challenging for me than Spartan races. These races make grown men and women cry. For example, there are over twenty-five grueling obstacles in Utah's Spartan Super—not something you get up and do well without training. It's not enough just to be in shape. People with conditioning often find themselves walking to the finish line. I've seen more people than I can count drop to the ground because of cramps or pure exhaustion. I've seen people vomit mid-race. I've seen life flights on the mountain picking up athletes who could not withstand the two-thousand-foot uphill climb over eight miles or the blistering July heat.

My first Utah Spartan was what they call the Beast, thirteen miles on a mountain with over thirty obstacles. I trained a little and got humbled. It took me three and a half hours to complete, and I was useless for a week. The humiliation I felt as I went from Unconscious Incompetence to Conscious Incompetence motivated me to train harder and give it another go, even though the race switched from a Beast to a Super. Every year since, I have worked harder and harder in the Conscious Competence stage. One year, I shaved twenty minutes off my previous year's best.

But I am a long way from Unconscious Competence, as I learned the next year, making too many mistakes on the obstacles toward the end. I still replay that spear throw in my mind. The obstacle is to throw the spear ten yards out into a stack of hay. You only get one shot at it, and I had never missed it. But I was a lot stronger with all the training I had been doing, and I overthrew it. Because I failed the obstacle, I had to do thirty burpees (you start on your feet and drop down on the ground to your stomach then back up to your feet again) before moving on in the race. It killed my time.

Moving forward, my goal is to complete a Spartan without failing an obstacle, getting to the point where the entire race is done with Unconscious Competence. But I never will if I don't continue to put in the work and keep my ego in check.

Spartan races are a lot like business and life. There are ups and downs. There are pitfalls and triumphs. Life can be hard for sure, but when you work hard toward a goal and achieve it, there is nothing so fulfilling as that accomplishment. Finishing the race, whether I fail an obstacle or not, feels good. It builds confidence even when I fall short. And we will all fall short. But what happens next? Do you shrink? Continue to fail because you stop learning? Only then can obstacles overcome you. The beauty of it is that you can get back up and start over again. Obstacles and adversity in general give us experience. We become stronger from them if we so choose. Failure is one of the greatest opportunities we have to learn, because we often feel it most acutely. No one becomes or stays great and keeps winning moments without drive, focus, and continued learning in Unconscious Competence.

DO THE WORK, PAY THE PRICE, MAKE MAGIC

Ego thrives in the path of least resistance, whereas a treasure trove of wisdom, humility, and great learning awaits those willing to pay the price to get where they want to be. You are not as good as you think you are. In many cases, not even close. Do not just pretend to do the work. Paying the price means doing whatever it takes to achieve your goal. Ego is more to blame for your quitting than your success. In failure, ego convinces you that the work is too hard or that you were not cut out to do that kind of work. This is why most people never get past Conscious Incompetence. They don't want to do the work. They won't get their hands dirty planting the seeds of their success.

The law of the harvest is straightforward: If you nurture and continuously care for the seed you have planted in good soil with water and plenty of sun, it will grow and, in time, bear fruit so that you may reap what you sow. But even though you provide the same care and attention to all of your seeds, each will grow differently, and the amount of fruit will vary. Some seeds will grow but not bear fruit. Some seeds may not grow at all.

In business, the same truth holds: Other people who do the same amount of work as you may experience more or less success planting and harvesting similar seeds. But what is that to you? Don't worry about them. Don't let ego breed envy in your heart. Instead, choose to celebrate their success, and let it give you hope for your own success as you stay focused on all that you can do. Remember, you must do the work and keep doing it until harvest. That's the only constant you can count on: What you reap may vary, but if you do not sow, you will not reap at all.

Even more tragic, many meaningful moments in the service of others will never be realized. As we face obstacles and adversity in our path and work our way through them, we will learn lessons we did not anticipate. Our thoughts and actions, the decisions we make, and the ways we choose to behave are what ultimately shape our character and destiny. We are agents that can independently act, making each of us solely responsible for who we are and what we become.

I know I may sound contrarian to the "do what you love" concept here, but it doesn't matter how much you love what you do if you do not have something bigger than you that drives it. In fact, I'd rather have a driven worker who works with purpose than a brilliant trainer who is passionate about training but uncommitted to the company's collective end goal. Passionate people may show some excitement at first but burn out because our common purpose does not resonate with them. Passion is not enough. A company with a collective purpose that drives their efforts will always outlast passionate individual effort.

I have hired my best employees following this rule; I always hire the ones who are willing to pay the price every day, no matter how hard the work may be, how long it takes, or how much they're being paid to do it. Why? Because they believe that the work they are doing will help the team reap what it sows. Don't just hire passionate people. Hire people who believe in you and who want to be a part of what you are doing for others.

If you are caught unaware, ego will convince you to quit or do less than your best. Doing your best work, whether you like the job you are doing or not, pays off in ways you may not currently see. It is like magic. Things just fall into place. Doors open that you may not currently anticipate. When the opportunity comes, you're ready, having done the work. That's what I have experienced in my career.

By choosing to always be a student, you will maintain your edge in your profession. You will develop the confidence necessary to be successful and stifle ego, knowing that there is always more to learn. Mastery for you has become a journey, not a destination. Only those who stay obsessed with what they do understand that the more they learn, the more they realize they do not know.

Your ego may tell you that you've arrived. This is a lie. There is always more to learn, no matter what you're doing or how long you have done it. Sound reason and acumen are accrued line upon line and precept upon precept. It comes a little at a time, and as you continue to strive in your learning, your understanding will increase. When you believe you have figured it out, the knowledge and understanding you have acquired with countless hours of work lose their edge. Without realizing it, your knowledge, understanding, and acumen begin to subtly but surely decline.

Sometimes this means that you'll need to get creative and discover new ground that has not yet been reached by anyone in your industry, field, or line of work. Choosing to forgo ego by becoming a constant student of your work makes you confident and self-assured in your ability to truly work at the highest level when others can only pretend.

Don't let ego fool you. When we get into our heads and play out all of the what-ifs before work begins or the price is paid, we end up focusing too much on those what-ifs. We lose the present moment. That's when you miss opportunities. To see them and win the moments we discussed in the last chapter, you must learn to be self- and socially aware in the present moment. Stay focused on why you do the work you're doing, and the *how* will present itself. Pay the price to learn how to win every moment that comes your way.

You can keep your ego in check by learning to cognitively separate yourself from events as they occur, good or bad. Learn to live independently of circumstance. As you learn to discipline yourself in this way, it will help you keep ego at bay, because you'll see yourself and others as equals—without rank or file. It also will not absolve you from taking responsibility for your actions. You exercise your agency and take a path that leads to success or failure. Agency empowers you to choose the path, but what you cannot choose is the consequence. Like it or not, you are responsible for your actions, which create the consequences that come as a result.

That said, your actions and their consequences do not have to make you the person that you are or that you are becoming. When you choose to learn from failure or a moment lost, you become a new creature, something entirely different than what you were before. You can choose to learn from your successes, too, although failure seems to be a much better teacher in many cases. We are human, which means we have the ability to win plenty of moments. It also means that losing moments is part of the program. We're going to make mistakes. But we can choose to learn from those mistakes, which will make us stronger than we were before those moments were lost. Once you choose to go down a path, whether that path is based on principle or derived from temporary emotion, you can begin to learn from your experience. Each action you take in a moment separates the "you" you are becoming from the "you" you were before the moment was lost.

This correct use of your agency is character building—it will help you become more complete and content as a person.

This change- and growth-driven mind-set, in and of itself, is the road less traveled. It will give you the ability to see yourself and others in a new light. We are people who do dumb things from time to time, but that does not make us dumb people. No matter how dumb or ill-advised our actions might have been up until this point in our lives, we are still capable of greatness. As long as we breathe, we can learn, grow, and progress. This is truth derived from confidence that will help you see yourself and others as equals—truth that will help you live an extraordinary life. Remember: Agency is the power to choose, and there are too many stories of people who chose to stop working at being great after they arrived at the top. So check your ego, and get to work. That's the best remedy for any doubt or obstacle.

Don't quit. Do your best work. And never, ever stop learning.

CHAPTER 6

FREEDOM FROM FORGETFULNESS

In 2017, my fifteen-year-old daughter, Fé, dropped an emotional bombshell on me during a therapy session. Fé is a deep sleeper and had been struggling to get out of bed in the mornings and to keep her room clean. She was also eating too much junk food. These were big changes from the way she had grown up; all of it and more was beginning to affect our relationship. I was worried something was wrong and felt she needed to talk to someone. We met with the therapist together first. That's when it happened.

Therapist: "How do you feel about your relationship with your dad?"

Fé: "I feel that my dad does not care about me."

I have heard my daughter say a version of this many times. Many parents have, especially when it comes to teenagers. It almost always happens during heated moments and arguments—in moments of anger, not in calm environments like this, while we were sitting down and had our wits about us, which is why the words hit me so hard.

My daughter was being sincere, but I was hurt and became defensive. *How could she feel this way?*

I have never been one of those dads who sits back and watches the process of growing up. I was there when she was born, and I cut the cord. I sang happy birthday to her in that moment and have been actively engaged ever since. How could she think that *I don't care?* She took her first steps toward me. I have hugged, kissed, and cuddled her more than anyone! *Of course I care.* I have bought her every piece of clothing she owns and the food she eats and the bed she sleeps in. *Would a person who made all of that happen not care for her?*

I tried to keep the shock I felt off my face as the therapist asked my daughter why she felt that way.

"When I tell him about my day, he seems uninterested. I told him that I got all As in school last week, and he barely even congratulated me. My dad and I would often cuddle and talk before I went to bed each night when I was young. Last week, I asked him how I looked after spending half the day getting ready for a school dance. He was walking up the stairs as I was walking down to go to the dance. He said I looked great and to have fun without even looking at me. He's just not there for me like he once was. He doesn't care."

I teach others to recognize that they are in the moment and to act on them to win those moments accordingly. By winning moments, we win at life. Apparently, I was not just losing moments with my daughter, I was failing miserably.

As I replayed over and over again throughout the day what Fé had said during the therapy session, I recalled voicemails I would get from my seventeen-year-old, Bela. She would say, "Dad, why don't you ever answer when I call?" Then I thought of Isaac, who would repeatedly say, "Dad! Dad! Dad!" from the backseat of my car until I would finally—agitatedly—respond. Even Hagen, who seems to care the least if you give him any attention at all, has moments when he wants to play, swing, or be tickled. How many of those moments had I missed? These were moments I did not even realize I was in.

Fé was wrong that I didn't care. I care deeply. But I can't deny that she felt that way. Were there other things I was doing at the time that I thought were more important? Not really. Maybe I got caught up now and then, but not as a rule. So what was it? What kept me from even recognizing—let alone winning—these moments?

The answer was as simple as it was pathetic to admit: I had forgotten to put aside "me" and pay attention—really listen—to those in my life who matter most.

LISTEN, OR YOU'LL MISS THE MOMENTS

How had I forgotten to pay attention to my kids? How does anyone fail to be completely present in the most important moments, or how could I be so invested in some seemingly "big" moments and yet completely ignore the small, everyday moments? Pretty easily, actually, and you might find that you do it more often than you realize. Getting caught up in triviality means we ignore opportunities or—worse—become hard of hearing toward those we work so hard to care for, as if any amount of success outside the home could compensate for that failure.

But it's not just at home; we—all of us—have a human tendency to focus on the events that affect us immediately rather than those moments that matter most. Like Captain Naaman (2 Kings 5), we wait to do some big thing while setting the many seemingly small and simple things aside. As a result, *our moments are lost at work and at home because we forget to listen.*

Just about every parent I know has told me that they wish they had spent more time with their kids. They all wish they had been less uptight or distracted, less *go, go, go.* They wish they had seized the opportunities to listen.

But this is not true just with our children and other personal and family relationships. In any occupation, active listening is key to effective teaching and persuasion. The ability to listen helps us stay focused on what is important to others. So often, we dismiss others' concerns or pass judgment before actually listening to what they are saying. By listening first and letting those around us know that we are listening, we begin to understand and bridge the gap between our differences so we can effectively work together to smash common goals and win moments that lead to business growth.

Moments are lost because we forget to do just that: be present and listen. Not just with our ears but with our eyes—like making eye contact when your daughter asks you how she looks, not just automatically saying she looks great. But it starts with our ears.

HOW TO LISTEN

As they say, the first step in solving a problem is recognizing you have one. Most of us are not good listeners. Good listening is an acquired skill; most of us may have working ears, but we don't know how to use them.

Studies show that we need to work at listening if only because we retain less auditory information than that from our other senses. For example, a study by Amy Poremba, now a program director at the National Institute on Deafness and a former psychology and neuroscience professor at the University of Iowa, had undergraduates listen to sounds, look at images, and hold objects with their hands. The students were then asked to recall the sounds, images, and objects an hour, a day, and a week later. The auditory stimuli recall came in last. According to Poremba, "Our auditory memory isn't as robust as we might like to think it is."[1]

Great, so we don't remember to listen or recall what we hear. How do we become present in a moment and improve our auditory recall? Some answers are just common sense:

★ Face the person speaking to you.

* Maintain eye contact.

* Be attentive but relaxed.

* Be open-minded to what is being said.

* Picture what is being said in your mind so you can better retain the information.

* Don't interrupt in casual conversation (as fun as that might be) or try to impose your point of view while others are speaking.

* Ask clarifying questions when the person speaking pauses so you can fully understand what is being said.

* Pay attention to what is *not* being said but is communicated through nonverbal messaging—body language, tone of voice, and expression.

But that list is incomplete, because knowing *what* needs to be done does not reflect the hard work and commitment involved in *consistently doing* those things to break the bad listening habits we already have. In other words, these things may be common sense, but they are not easy to do—especially if we don't first make the active choice to listen.

You must practice your ability to listen for opportunities when they come. Customers have problems they can't solve. People continue in old, worn-out routines because they do not know better. They just keep grinding away, doing what they do, until you show them there is a better way. You will not solve their headaches or be able to create hope for them until you start listening to them.

Simply put, we have to want to listen. It is a choice we make every day and in every moment. Without that choice and the sense of purpose that comes with it to drive us to be better listeners, we will likely forget to do the work that it takes. Choosing not to listen means choosing not to recognize moments when they occur, genuinely and fully. Remember: We win moments by living truth, which will help us live happy and fulfilled lives. Great listening keeps us from caving to the tendency of ignoring what's most important.

JUST. STOP. TALKING.

My friend Scott, a successful entrepreneur, had gotten to a point in life where he could afford to build a big, beautiful new home. One morning, while touring the still-under-construction new home with his younger daughter, Grace, he noticed something he hadn't before: One area upstairs had a great view of the surrounding area.

As Scott looked at the view, he said, "We are going to have to do something really special with this area, so everyone and our guests can regularly enjoy it."

His daughter was incensed. "Oh no!" she exclaimed angrily. "This is my area!" She then made it clear that she felt she deserved the bedroom of her choice.

"You don't deserve anything!" Scott snapped. But as the words came out of his mouth, he immediately realized that he had hurt his daughter's feelings and missed an opportunity to hear her out.

Once in the car, Scott asked Grace to tell him what she was feeling and thinking.

Her explanation was simple. She wanted a sanctuary. Although Scott was now happily married, he had gone through a divorce from the daughter's mother, which had been particularly painful for both his children. His daughter told him there had been so much change in her life the past few years that she just wanted a peaceful place to call her own.

Scott had been through a similar experience in his childhood. He explained that he understood her feelings and was able to relate, sharing his childhood experiences and feelings. He then used this moment to teach his daughter a bigger lesson about gratitude and

how blessed they were to be building this home. He knew that without having listened to her first, he would never have had this teaching moment, and if he had just shut his mouth and used his ears in the
first place, he would have also avoided the initial drama.

He figured out in that moment how to listen first and how to let
his daughter know that he was listening. Think about that the next
time one of your employees asks for something you think he or she
doesn't deserve. Before you start throwing stones, ask why, and
then choose to shut up and listen to what he or she has to say.

★

OPEN YOUR EARS—AND YOUR EYES

Fé told me two weeks ago that she is learning from me what not to do
when raising her kids. How's that for a kick in the back pockets? When
I think about some of the things my parents did that I have never
done, I can't help but relate to what she said. Our kids learn more
from what we do than what we say. The same is true in business—and
everywhere in life. The smallest things matter.

For example, say you need some copies. If your people see you
walk past the copier to ask someone else to do it, they'll follow your
example. It would have taken you the same time to copy it yourself, but
instead, you delegated to someone else—who likely has his or her own
work to do. Your employees may learn from you that it's OK to interrupt their coworkers for a simple task they could have done themselves.
Now imagine that you don't listen effectively. They will not only fail to
learn from you how to listen, but they may also think, subconsciously
or otherwise, that it is OK to not listen to others.

Effective listening is the cornerstone of great leadership and of all
our relationships. It unlocks the door to understanding and winning
moments. We should spend far more time listening than on any other

form of communication, but it is not something any of us learn in school; so we have to learn it ourselves, then pass it on to our teams. I have taken and seen countless introductory classes on speaking, writing, selling, marketing, and beyond—every aspect of business you can think of. Yet there's no Listening 101. And even if there were, I wonder how many would truly grasp the social advantage they would have with listening mastery.

You have to lead—and parent—by example. Make sure your actions reflect the principles you have established in your organization. When you listen effectively and show others how to do it by the example you have set, they'll be much more likely to follow suit.

BUILDING A TEAM THAT LISTENS—AND IS LISTENED TO

With all that is at stake in business every day, you would be amazed by how much risk can be mitigated with the right team. But it doesn't matter how good your team may be if you don't listen when they speak. Even if you keep your ego in check, you may not realize that by not listening to your team, you are setting yourself up for failure—instead of success.

It's important that leaders realize that no one is a "jack of all trades" in this day and age. Although we may be fair or even good at many things, leaders who try to do them all are not great at any. As your company grows, excellence and expertise are no longer a "nice to have" in today's competitive job environment. They're a must! Even if you are a small to medium-size business owner, you need to give up certain jobs and narrow your responsibilities down to three (or fewer) key roles. You want to make sure you are the best in these areas of responsibility and that they leave you feeling fulfilled when you perform in them.

Once you have narrowed your responsibilities to three key roles, learn to eat, breathe, and sleep those key roles. Master them. Your mastery in these key areas will attract key people to you, so make sure you do them better than anyone you know—that you stand out as one with specific, uncommon ability. Once you have narrowed your key roles, you can begin hunting for talent to join your team and even outsource great talent. Your mastery in those few areas will attract talent to help in areas where you're not as strong.

Now you are set up for success through effective listening and by hiring others with specific expertise to help you run your company in the smartest, most efficient way possible. To practice listening to those key players, you must first learn how to attract them to your business.

It has been my experience as a business owner that if you are a confident—not egotistical—person, you are already open and willing to listen. You are also able to present your company purpose in a way that appeals to others and draw influential people to you and your cause over time. But you'll be better able to retain these key players on your team if you take these four steps in the following order once you hire them:

★ Ensure that each key player believes in the company's purpose or the reason behind what you do collectively and individually. Talented people are good, but a unified team is better.

★ Be open, willing to listen to their point of view, and even willing to make company course corrections based on what they, you, and the executive team as a whole agree upon.

★ Put your key players in positions where they can call the shots over their departments and can show great proficiency and a love for the specific work or role they play on your team.

★ Based on your company's means, compensate fairly.

When you have all the right common-purpose-driven players, that's when the magic happens. In this atmosphere, you can tackle challenges and experience collective ownership of the agreed-upon solutions. Once a plan of action is created and clearly understood, there will be little to no need for supervision. Your team will not care how long the work takes or how hard the work is or how much they are being paid to do it. They'll just take ownership and do it. This sense of ownership is crucial when tackling problems, creating solutions, and considering company direction. That way, you don't have to do everything yourself or even weigh in on everyday decisions.

LISTENING IN PRACTICE

Now, I fully admit I failed to do this in my company in the past and made my share of unilateral decisions, which have cost the company money and some really talented people. I absolutely regret those boneheaded ideas I've tried to carry out on my own instead of allowing people with different skill sets take ownership in decision making with me. But the only way that distributed responsibility works in a company is with intense active listening, in one-on-one meetings, and especially around the table in group settings.

My company has "roundtable" meetings twice a year. At these retreats, we endeavor to connect with each member on the executive team by becoming present with their expression, tone, and intent. In other words, we really try to learn to shut our mouths and let others speak during these meetings—to be fully engaged, to put our phones down. The email or text you just received likely can wait. Just breathe, relax, quiet the chatter in your brain, and do not let a word come out of your mouth. Just maintain eye contact except when taking notes, and continue to actively listen.

★ Don't get offended.

★ Don't be quick to disagree.

★ Don't interrupt.

★ Don't get distracted by whatever else is going
on in the room or in your mind.

What you want to say is never as important as showing the person who is speaking that they are worthy of your attention. Stop longing to hear the sound of your own voice. Only when others at the roundtable are done talking can you open your mouth, and then only to ask questions to clarify any points made and ask if there is anything else they wanted to add. This is not idle chitchat; this is the group of people you have entrusted to run your company—to do what you were born in this world to do. But don't think about that, or you'll forget to listen.

So many tangible results have come out of our company executive retreats that I can't even count them. Because it is a safe environment, we can be frank and speak openly about common challenges. The best part about getting together during these meetings is that we are able to create structure around the continued growth and success of our company—not just new processes and procedures, but further refinement of our company mission, purpose, and core values. These are what drive us to fight through any obstacle and do whatever it takes to see more opportunity and win more moments.

There are moments filled with opportunity all around us. We need the capacity to meet those opportunities through listening. Once our capacity to actively listen has been developed, we are present in moments when they occur, and there's no limit to what doors we can open.

To win more moments, learn to *listen* and be ready for them.

CHAPTER 7

FREEDOM FROM INDIFFERENCE

W hen Phil received the news of his employee Patty's resignation
and the harsh criticism in her email, he was conflicted. In the
email, Patty had written how Phil had treated her with disrespect, how
she had grown tired of not living up to his expectations, and how her
request for a review and a raise had been repeatedly ignored. Finally,
she wrote that Phil was dishonest and did not abide by the company's
principles. She just couldn't take it anymore.

On one hand, Phil was relieved. He had put off Patty's request for
a review because he did not feel she deserved a raise; he had even been
considering firing her for months now. Patty had once been a hard
worker with a great attitude. But during the last few months, her behavior had become increasingly indifferent. She was disengaged and distant in her communication. She remained somewhat responsible and
completed most of her duties, but it was easy to see that her heart was
no longer in it. More than that, Patty's fellow employees began to notice
her discontent and lack of interest. They felt that she now wanted to
pass the buck and would become defensive and self-defeating when she
received feedback.

On the other hand, Phil had no idea where all of her harsh criticism of him had come from. Patty's letter of resignation clearly stated that she would accept no further contact whatsoever, but there were so many unanswered questions. What was it that Patty found so disrespectful? How had Phil been dishonest? In what ways did he not adhere to his founding principles (principles he had penned with his own hand)? He thought about what Patty called her "final straw": a text in which he had asked Patty why she continued to ignore his request that she complete a specific task that he believed was within her scope of responsibility. Certainly, that was not something to quit over.

Why had a good worker with a fine attitude like Patty become increasingly disengaged? Why had she felt disrespected? What Phil did not recognize was that his own indifference toward Patty and her request for a review had caused this sad tale.

IT'S EASY TO SPOT

You might argue that Patty's email was the opposite of indifferent; it was full of pent-up rage exploding after months—or years—of silent pressure. But her frustration should have been clear from her work performance. A once competent and enthusiastic employee who becomes disconnected from her duties and coworkers is a sign of something under the surface— unhappiness, boredom, anger, or some other form of aggravation.

Anna Maravelas, a licensed psychologist and consultant who works with companies and leaders to restore trust, resolve conflict, and improve productivity around the world, sees indifference and apathy as a defeatist attitude that comes with a lack of energy. People are clock watching and doing just enough to keep their jobs, and some eventually end up like Patty. "People either check out or become over-concerned with their breaks and vacations," Maravelas says.[1]

Jayne Jenkins, CEO at the executive coaching company Churchill Leadership Group, says that when apathy in the workplace sets in, individuals may become disengaged, which has a direct effect on the company's bottom line.[2]

Bob Ruotolo, an organizational development consultant, author, and speaker, talks about how apathetic people can come across as "detached, unfocused, without much of an attention span. Their energy may be low. They may be easy to anger, argumentative, or defensive."[3]

Samuel Culbert, an author and a professor of management at UCLA, notes that you can simply "look at the [employee's] face. People who don't care look like they don't care."[4] Can't picture it? Just think back on your last experience working with the lovely government workers at the DMV, and you'll know what I mean.

Indifference occurs when people believe their talents are not being used to their potential. It happens when employees are fearful and worried about their own job security. Indifference rears its ugly head when there is conflict between leaders and the team. And it results from less-than-favorable working conditions, where no one feels safe to speak freely. Indifference deeply affects morale and can cause employees to disconnect.

If you don't know what is causing your employee to distance herself, ask! The only way to solve a problem is to find out what it is, then find a way to fix it. Do not put it off until later. Do not ignore it. Fix it right now.

DO SOMETHING ABOUT IT!

As Patty's boss, Phil should have seen this coming. In fact, he *did* see it coming, but he didn't do anything about it. He is the one we're focused on here, the one who can keep Patty from making an abrupt exit. But putting off a simple request from an employee, ignoring that he had her doing something she was unhappy with, unsuited for, or currently neglecting, didn't make those problems go away. It only made the situation worse, and it eventually led down a path to a dead end from which there was no return.

Too often, we don't follow through, and we fail to find the truth that can help us grow and become better even against the biggest challenges. If we are not careful, ego can and will creep in, and we'll refuse to listen and blame others for our problems. The result of all that can make us become indifferent, especially to people like Patty, and they, in turn, become indifferent to us.

★

CHOOSE TO CARE

In September 1946, after her retreat at the Loreto Convent, Sister Teresa felt compelled to leave the comforts of her home to live among the poor. She said that in that moment she felt the impression "that was a call within a call." To not obey it in her mind would be to break her faith.

Two years later, Sister Teresa chose her experience in a most literal fashion. She took on Indian citizenship, received basic medical training, and ventured into the slums of Calcutta, where she quickly found herself begging for food. She experienced loneliness and doubt that made going back to her convent a tempting proposition. She wrote in her diary about the adversity she felt during those first months living among the poor and the needy:

> I learned a good lesson today. The poverty of the poor
> must be so hard for them. While looking for a home
> I walked and walked till my arms and legs ached. I
> thought how much they must ache in body and soul,
> looking for a home, food and health. Then, the comforts
> of Loreto came to tempt me. "You have only to say the

word and all that will be yours again," the Tempter kept on saying. Of free choice, my God, and out of love for you, I desire to remain and do whatever be your Holy will in my regard. I did not let a single tear come.[6]

Sister Teresa became known around the world as Mother Teresa—now Saint Teresa—for her empathy for the poor and the needy. She left the comforts of her home to live and care for them, on the streets of Calcutta and in the leper colonies in Yemen. She courageously stepped outside of her emotions to clearly see the perspective and worth of others. What followed was a life lived extraordinarily with many years of moments won.

We can do the same without sacrificing anything close to what Sister Teresa did. We can imagine the best possible outcomes in our hearts instead of caving to hurtful emotions that make us overly critical of ourselves and others. Contempt can be subdued as we accept that we all are equal and of great worth. Defensiveness can dissipate as we put our emotions aside to understand others without necessarily agreeing with them. The stonewalling in our relationships can stop when we courageously begin to communicate and share what we are feeling in our relationships.

As we consciously create common ground, we can overcome the emotions that hurt us. By choosing to care regardless of how much it may hurt, we give others the opportunity to connect and become present because we have shown genuine empathy and respect for their worth.

Let your empathy for others help you act on truth. By choosing to care, you choose to think about what you are thinking. You choose to control how you feel independently of circumstances. You can overcome the tendency to be indifferent by choosing your experience independently of circumstance, occurrences, and your emotions in any given situation. As you learn to do this, you will forgo your tendency to stop caring, and you will win moment after moment.

★

Patty had one big reason for her resignation: She had been asking for a review and a raise for a while, since before her performance had declined. Phil had chosen to stonewall those requests—indifference and inaction—instead of addressing the issue head-on, which caused the situation to deteriorate further. Everything else came as a result of Phil's inaction. Patty becoming emotionally disconnected and her harsh criticism, contempt, and defensive behavior helped justify her decision to move on, but only because she felt Phil's seeming indifference toward her requests for a review. The months of disconnection that cost Phil money, morale, and hurt feelings could have been avoided with communication—a heartfelt review in which both Phil and Patty could address their concerns openly and find a solution.

That solution did not necessarily have to be that Patty continued in her position. There were so many other positive outcomes to consider. Patty might have convinced Phil that she deserved a raise or could have regained his confidence that she would re-engage in her duties. Phil could have explained his concerns with her performance. He could also have agreed that improved emotional engagement from Patty over a mutually agreed-upon period could lead to the requested raise. Even dismissal could be considered a winning moment if both parties had ended up with a more positive outcome than Patty's abrupt resignation.

We can only imagine now how much more effective it would have been to create a safe environment for clear and honest communication from both parties. Patty and Phil could have reasoned with one another, communicated more productively, and come to a resolution. Even if she had still ended up leaving the position, the separation would have been on more amicable terms.

Every one of us has felt the remorse or embarrassment that comes from making a mistake—not just from actions done wrong but also from actions left undone. Sometimes the resulting pain in our conscience can hurt far worse than physical pain. Apathy and indifference stifle your conscience. In this manner, indifference is like a strong drink. When you choose to become indifferent, you grow numb. You stop caring and become far too comfortable ignoring the truth. To remain in this stupor is dangerous, because remorse and pain of conscience are your body's emotional response, trying to make you aware that something needs to change—that *you* need to change!

Indifference sows the seeds of criticism, contempt, defensiveness, and stonewalling. Apathy is the great enabler in the demise of our relationships in business, as well as at home. *Things* do not cause problems. *People* do when they choose not to care. But people can also work to correct those problems by choosing to care and thus becoming heroes over indifference.

THINK ABOUT WHAT YOU ARE THINKING

You may not realize it, but you talk to yourself all the time. That inner dialogue is called *self-talk*. It engages your emotions and can manipulate your view of reality to keep you from being your best self.

It is often easier to blame someone or something else instead of taking responsibility for our actions and how we choose to feel. But that blame doesn't change the truth: We are, in fact, responsible for our reactions. This is particularly true when we self-talk ourselves into believing we are victims. No one but us can control how we choose to focus, think, feel, and respond to what happens to us. If we are not actively aware, our self-talk can create an emotional response that betrays our better judgment, and we will point the finger at everyone and everything outside of ourselves for how we have chosen to think and feel.

But self-talk is not just about blame. It's about convincing yourself you are so right that you become indifferent to what others might be thinking. It is so much easier to walk away from situations like these than to face them head-on. Remember, Phil was *relieved* that Patty walked away from their relationship. It kept him from having to take action. But we have the power to think about what we are thinking, and we can change what we are thinking to change how we feel.

Johnny Covey (Stephen R. Covey's grandnephew) is an accomplished speaker and author. According to his book *5 Habits to Lead from Your Heart*, we can choose our experience by learning to become aware of what we are thinking and feeling in real time. When we respond negatively to what we think and feel, Covey calls this "being in your head." That can lead to panic or feeling like we're trapped in a situation, making us feel wrong, alone, or unworthy, which triggers our fight-or-flight mode. As a result, we either seek to control our environment through force, or we retreat to short-term, numbing outlets that create temporary comforts (such as sex, drugs, and alcohol). But control and comfort are remedies with a short shelf life. As we seek control or retreat to momentary comforts, argues Covey, we choose to ignore what our conscience is trying to tell us. By becoming self-aware in a moment, we can see what we are experiencing and begin to cognitively construct a new and much more appealing internal experience.[5]

My son Isaac taught me a lesson that helps illustrate this point. I had planned a date with my wife. All I needed to do was get Isaac off to wrestling practice, but Isaac was tired and didn't want to go. I managed to get him to the car and drove him to practice. The entire ride, he wasn't happy and did not talk much.

It took forever to convince him to get out of the car when we arrived. I even had to walk him into the wrestling room, where all the other kids were busy practicing. Isaac stopped at the door and told me again that he didn't want to go. I knew that if I didn't get home soon, the babysitter would arrive at the house before I got back, so I grabbed Isaac by the arm and said, "Yes you are," and I pushed him into practice.

As soon as I turned around to walk back outside, I felt a shadow behind me. It was Isaac, now more determined than ever to not go to practice.

Then I stopped and thought about what I was thinking. Force was obviously a bad idea, and it didn't work the first time, so I tried threatening him: "If you don't go to practice today, you will not compete on Saturday," I said.

"I don't care," Isaac replied.

I struggled to let my love for my son tame the angry emotion I was feeling in the moment. It's important to accept that Isaac was not making me feel anything. He does not have that power unless I give it to him. I was concerned about the babysitter and the date with my wife. My self-talk was creating my heated emotions, creating that fight-or-flight response and affecting my better judgment. In that moment, I was not thinking about what Isaac needed. Any poor action I took while in this state of mind would be my fault, not his.

I turned to Isaac and crouched down on one knee. I didn't want to come across as overbearing or pushy for fear that Isaac's fight-or-flight mode would kick back in and cloud his judgment too.

I waited until his eyes caught mine. "Son," I said, "why don't you want to go to wrestling practice?"

He put his head down, and he said, "I'm tired, and I don't want to be here."

I responded, "I know you're tired, buddy, and you don't want to be here today. When we talked about the work you needed to do in practice last Tuesday in order to compete, you agreed, did you not?" I asked.

With his chin still on his chest, he slowly responded, "Yes."

"You made a commitment, son, and we do not back out on our commitments even when we're tired," I said. "Now, you may not think it is a big deal to miss practice every now and again, but there is something much bigger that I am trying to teach you. If you do not learn to keep your commitments now, while you're young, you will face much harsher consequences when you get older. Whether it is commitments you make at work or at home, others will trust you to do your part. I am trying to help you learn this lesson now so you don't have to experience the hurt you might cause yourself or others later on in life. Now you have a choice to make, son. You can go back home with me now and face the consequence of not being able to compete on Saturday, or you can walk in that wrestling room even though you're tired and practice today. So, what's it going to be?"

I let no emotion show on my face as I stood there looking at Isaac and waiting for him to decide.

Isaac brought his hands up level with his head, his fingers spread apart. His open palms were facing his ears without touching and his elbows were pinned to his ribs. He put his chin down to his chest and closed his eyes while slowly taking a deep breath. He seemed to be processing everything—thinking about what he was thinking. He then took a step forward, which created enough momentum to propel him back into the wrestling room. The coach tapped him on the shoulder, gave him a reassuring grin, and found him a wrestling partner as I left.

On the drive back home, the lesson was clear in my mind. In fight-or-flight mode, we see nothing clearly. I was so determined to make him go to practice that I made it feel like my life depended on it. He was not going to be forced to practice, and he acted as if his life depended on it too. By stopping my own self-talk, I transitioned my focus to what was most important—Isaac. I had to show my son I cared about him more than getting back before the babysitter arrived. Doing so opened a window of opportunity where he could consider what I was trying to teach him and freely make a choice for himself.

By paying attention to my son and myself in this one interaction, I became much more self- and socially aware. I was able to see what was really going on and make course corrections in that moment. I lost the indifference I was feeling and gained influence with my son.

Simply put, fight-or-flight emotion is the body's instinctive reaction to what is occurring around or inside of us. As we cognitively press pause and think about what we are feeling, we can begin to interpret the meaning of our emotions. While in this creative state of mind, we can imagine the best possible outcome and respond accordingly. Covey calls this strong state of self-awareness "being in your heart." It is how you proactively choose your experience, and this gives you the ability to mentally press that pause button while in a moment.

Consider where your focus is right now. Think about what it is you are thinking and the emotions your body is creating as a reaction to the self-talk or thoughts going on inside your head. By doing this, you can cognitively press pause on that self-talk and determine what is missing in any given moment, consciously uncover the right answer based on the truth (what is right), and respond accordingly. This mental practice will help you become more self-aware and strengthen your emotional intelligence. As you develop an ability to choose your experience, you'll win more moments and even discover more truth. The application of truth opens the door to continued learning and progress, whereas caving to tendency impedes continued learning and progress.

EMPLOYEE SATISFACTION

Workplace indifference is destructive. One of the main reasons employees stop caring about the work they do is because they feel their leaders do not care about them. As a leader, if you do not show you care about those around you, they will soon begin to wonder whether they can trust you. This human tendency toward indifference wreaks havoc on relationships everywhere in our lives.

Your employees are the most valuable asset you have in your

organization, and its performance depends on their individual efforts. When your employees buy in to what you are doing, the purpose behind your company, they're not just more content at work; they work harder, independent of pay, no matter how hard the job may be or how long the work takes. This extra effort propels company growth. People believe that what they're doing is important—bigger than they are—because you've shown them that it *is* important.

Your business is not about things; it is about people. Your people—your employees—take care of your customers. Those people you think are your customers are actually your employees' customers. Your employees deal with them directly; your team drives the customer experience.

Think back to what I said at the start of this book: Your customers will choose a company that gives them a great experience over brand or price. The same holds true for your inside customers—your employees. Be sure to treat your employees the way you want them to treat their customers. The level of their emotional engagement and ultimate success at work depends more on their work conditions and overall experience than the product or service you are selling. If your employees do not feel that you care about them, they may stop caring about you, like Patty did. And if they stop caring about you, they may care less about your customers, and you know where that leads.

The goal is for employees to perform their individual responsibilities in accordance with their unique strengths and skill sets. Putting them in a position with a set of responsibilities based on their strengths will enable you to emotionally let go and become free to work on the business. Make sure you have the right talent in the right seats, and treat your people the way you want your customers to be treated. That's how you minimize the spread of workplace apathy and grow your business with people who care.

The best leaders hire for attitude, train for talent, and ask for excellence. Because your performance expectations are so high, you are also responsible in part to improve your people's capacity to do the work you expect them to do. Find the best training money can buy for every role on your team, and give your people the skill sets they need to excel in their chosen roles by continually making sure it is implemented. Once you and each person on your team uncover their strengths, understand how they can best contribute in your company, and have the tools to succeed, you can demand even more excellence in the responsibilities they have been given.

By taking these steps, you will show that you care about them and their success and individual growth in your company, and they'll care more about the collective growth of the company and take better care of your—*their*—customers.

CHAPTER 8

FREEDOM FROM SELFISHNESS

The other day I was listening to one of my clients' calls with a service agreement customer looking to receive service on his furnace before the weather turned too cold. The call was going well until the call handler told the customer that he did not have an opening until January. If the call had been in July and the wait until September, that would have been all fine and good, but this was the first of November—nearly furnace weather already. To get his system serviced, the client would have to wait until the winter was half over.

I don't know about you, but I would not be happy waiting more than two months to get a service I had already paid for so my family would not run the risk of freezing in the dead of winter. A couple of weeks? Fine. But two months? I get that busy season is my client's bread and butter, but how does that happen?

Did it happen because they hadn't thought about their customers when they needed to, and now the customer was an inconvenience? A simple call before the busy season hit would have been easy to make and might have gotten the service done before the client even remembered to ask—and before the winter rush. Did anyone send an email or text reminder? Did they ask to schedule the off-season clients for the same time each year when they sold them the maintenance contract or first serviced their system? This would have made the process easy for the customer so they wouldn't even have to think about it.

This would have made it easier on my client too; they wouldn't be bogged down with contract customers during their peak period, and they would lose fewer of those contracts.

The last thing you should do is make a customer feel less important because of all the cash you are making elsewhere. The goal should be to create a balance in your workflow year-round by being as proactive as possible before each busy season hits. Find a way to make every customer feel special, regardless of when you deliver on the promise you made. That's where meaningful moments begin.

★

NO, REALLY, THE WORLD DOES NOT REVOLVE AROUND YOU

Nicolaus Copernicus was a sixteenth-century Polish mathematician who changed everything we thought we knew about our place in the universe. He taught that the earth revolved around the sun. Before his thinking became accepted as truth, we believed that the planets and stars revolved around Earth. While the world now accepts what Copernicus taught about our planet, too many of us still think the world revolves around us. *And we take for ourselves first.*

When we take, we are looking out for number one regardless of the collateral damage. We tend to put the truth aside to justify our actions. In other words, the truth takes a backseat to self-centered tendencies, causing us to shrink and lose moments, even when we think we've won.

That's what happened with me and that race with Coach Garcia. But it isn't in competition that we lose ourselves in ourselves;

it happens every day in the littlest moments, not the big ones, that bring out the best or worst in us.

Take driving, for example: Ever pushed the gas to fly through a light just as it changes? Tailgated someone because they were not going as fast as we thought they should? Failed to realize you were exceeding the speed limit in the left lane? Honked at someone even though they had the right of way? Ignored the "No Turn on Red" sign? Swung a quick lane change to get off at the exit you were about to miss instead of just going to the next one? Backed out of a parking spot without looking? Parked in one of the empty handicapped spots in front of a crowded store because you were "just running in for a minute"?

Here's one we've *all* done: double dipped a chip. I get it: You're not sick; you're the healthiest person you know. Oh, you did the flip and double dip so the other side that didn't touch your lips went into the salsa, and you washed your hands when you got to the party. Yeah, right.

Who are you thinking of in those situations? You're thinking of yourself. Copernicus showed us that we had been wrong about Earth's place in the universe. He said nothing about human tendency to believe it about ourselves. He shouldn't have to. We know better. Now we just need to do better.

★

WHAT GOES AROUND

Selfishness and power tend to go hand in hand and can be found at the core of any number of Hollywood, government, or corporate scandals broadcast in our media today. People use their position of power for self-gain and to dominate others. Why is it that when we accumulate a little knowledge, power, or influence, we immediately begin to use it to the detriment of others in order to assert and maintain that power, instead of using it to generate abundance as well as win-win scenarios?

Personal accomplishment can open doors with greater capacity to help and serve those around us. But what happens when the thickness of our heads and wallets takes precedence over people who need serving? This is when the collateral damage of taking instead of giving begins to pile on. Soon, if you're not careful, selfishness will render you morally bankrupt. Power, knowledge, and influence will open doors for sure, but if selfishness is left unchecked, it's like walking through a revolving door that will hit you square in the back.

I am not questioning that a little self-centeredness can be a strength. Why do you think flight attendants always remind us to put our own oxygen masks on first before helping those who can't? You can't save others if you lose yourself in the process. Or consider working out. When you take time regularly to work out and keep your body healthy, you'll feel better about yourself and have more energy to serve others. Overwhelmed by work? It's a good thing to unplug and refresh with some vacation time or even a day trip just for you. This kind of self-centeredness is fueled by self-awareness. It may be about creating a happy life and lifestyle for you, but it's also about leading by example or mentoring others to find their happy lifestyle. It's about having the power to live and serve, not live and screw everyone else.

Simply put, our actions often determine our fate. Whatever you do will come back to you. Selfishness has certainly taken its toll on all of us. It is not do unto others and take everything you want. It is do unto others *as you would have them do unto you.*

THE TRUTH ISN'T FLEXIBLE

Early in my career, I worked in sales at Ascend Marketing, a company that coaches small businesses in marketing, advertising, and sales. One day, I was pushing hard to impress the leadership there during a call. I had earned their trust, and I wanted to show them I was capable of earning and doing much more.

The prospective client had questions I did not know the answers to, but instead of saying "I don't know," I told them what I thought they wanted to hear. I thought I sounded impressive.

Jim Ackerman, the owner of Ascend, did not. He happened to be sitting in the next room while I was spewing balderdash, and when I got off the sales call, full of confidence that the prospect would close, he walked into my office. I put my hands behind my head and leaned back in my chair with a smug look on my face. I slowly turned my chair toward him.

Jim asked me how the call went. "Oh, pretty good," I said. "He'll close."

"Well, that puts you in a precarious situation," he responded. "What are you going to do when he finds out you stretched the truth about our offering?"

I played it coy, putting a confused look on my face, but Jim had none of it.

"I heard the call, Brigham," he said disappointedly. "When a client signs on with us, we're making an agreement with them. If they find out later that we've deceived them, they're not likely to stay with us. And they'll spread the word to other potential clients."

I leaned forward slowly in my chair and looked down at the ground sheepishly. "I will make sure I am clear on what is being offered before I let him close, Jim."

After a short silence, Jim let out a deep sigh and calmly said, "Brigham, I'm impressed with you. You have great capacity. But stretching the truth to make sales is not something we do here. Understood?"

I looked back up at him and agreed with a nod.

I felt like such a dunderhead. What was it that I was sacrificing by choosing to stretch the truth? I wanted to make a sale to impress Jim. Because of my self-centered desires, I had done just the opposite: I had lost a moment with the prospective client and Jim. I had also disappointed myself by failing to live by the truth. *When you are solely focused on your own best interest, you're setting yourself up for failure—failure that negatively affects everyone around you.*

This lesson plays itself out not just in our exaggeration of the truth or in outright lies, but in the holes we dig for ourselves by failing to consider others.

GET OVER YOURSELF AND GIVE

All the human tendencies we've covered so far—negativity, ego, not listening, and indifference—fuel self-centered behavior. Every act of selfishness turns a moment into a negative experience for everyone and reduces our social awareness. It leads to moments when it seems we aren't aware of the problem or concerned for others' happiness and well-being. In these moments, we are our own worst enemy. With every selfish act, you hurt everyone around you, especially yourself, because you'll destroy relationships, your credibility with others, and your own self-worth.

Selfish people always take, in big and small ways, by:

★ Sacrificing someone else's happiness or success for their own short-term gain

★ Building themselves up at the expense of others

★ Claiming credit for the work of others

★ Lying or stealing

★ Being rude, disdainful, and mean

★ Feeling satisfaction when others fail

★ Resenting the success of others, trivializing them, or actively working against their success

★ Preferring to expose others to public humiliation and claiming vindication as opposed to offering personal, heartfelt reconciliation

How frozen must your heart be to do these things actively (or passively) and be so blind to it? But you can overcome it by learning the power to give of yourself to others, by making choices that go beyond each customer transaction. Zig Ziglar said it well: "To get what you want, you need to help enough other people get what they want."[1] The desire to take only for ourselves first should not just be controlled. It should be annihilated. We all have the agency to build a life of meaningful experiences and long-term relationships. We do not have to grow up hardened by our own selfishness or the selfishness we have experienced from others. We can rise above it. We can look outside of ourselves to remind us of all the good that is and that we can do for those around us.

When I started my company back in 2008, my first client did not pay me a dime to train his call-handling team. I offered the service for free to save the online media advertising I was doing for him at the time. I had to prove that the online leads we generated for him were quality—meaning that he could make sales from them.

His team just needed training to learn how to book those kinds of leads. His team could make good use of the leads my advertising was generating because I would train them how at no cost. Only when I was willing to invest my time and give first to my client did this opportunity open the door to what is now a multimillion-dollar training and certification company.

Your work, like art, must be shared as often as possible in its imperfection and practiced over and over again, whether people see it or not—and even whether they pay you or not. When we go, go, go, we often just take, take, take—or worse, we give so we can take or get back. That's not heroic. That constant taking and expectation makes us our own worst enemies. Stop needing to be the center of it all. To be the hero, learn to give first—without condition, expectation, or fear. Jump on every opportunity to improve what you do and give. Give as much as you can as often as you can. When you learn to give and keep giving, you'll be amazed at how the world gives back—in time, talent, and treasure, but also in moments that go beyond anything that can be measured. To find meaning in your life, learn to give first to create memorable experiences and build long-term relationships.

CHAPTER 9

FREEDOM FROM FEAR

O n a business trip to Washington, DC, I found myself with some downtime and headed over to the National Mall. I made my way over to the Lincoln Memorial, and as I started up the steps, the words engraved on a broad landing drew me toward them. I pivoted to read them:

I HAVE A DREAM

MARTIN LUTHER KING, JR.

THE MARCH ON WASHINGTON

FOR JOBS AND FREEDOM

AUGUST 28, 1963

I stood there, fixated on those words and realizing that Dr. King had given his historic speech on this very spot. The Mall's reflecting pool and the Washington Monument stretched before me, and I was moved. I imagined myself standing there that day as Dr. King shared his dream. That night, I found myself reading and studying the civil rights movement, and realized I knew less than I thought about Dr. King and his nonviolent approach to civil rights.

Despite the hate launched at him and the resulting violence in the 1960s, Dr. King refused to live in fear or to return hate with hate. The more I studied his background and teachings, I came to realize that this nonviolent approach wasn't just a gimmick to attain equal rights: It was the true way, the right way to combat racism at the time. Dr. King didn't just *believe* that peace was the answer. He *knew* it was, and he endeavored to purge all animosity he felt toward his oppressors. He did not hate them—or fear them. It was quite the opposite. He loved them, and he did all he could to help them see what they were doing to themselves and how their hate and anger were actually crippling their ability to think clearly and love or forgive. Like the Baptist minister he was, he used his charisma and spellbinding ability to deliver a speech to try to make the world a better place for *ALL* people, not just those who looked like him. Dr. King is remembered for how he lived: unafraid to stand for what he believed was right and living by the truth.

We must also live by the truth if we want to live a life patterned after excellence. Running away from the things we fear and toward temporary pleasures—like when I made up stories about what my company offered just to land a sale, will cost us. Instead of pushing our limits while living in truth and winning moments, we find ourselves content to remain in our emotional famine. And when the thrill of that famine fades—like a drug—we seek the next temporary fix.

Living solely by sensations or to satisfy our appetites is no way to live, especially when there are far better and bigger causes waiting to fill us up in far more fulfilling ways. Great men like Dr. King are not remembered for their appetites, but rather for believing in and bravely living selflessly for causes far greater than themselves. Neal A. Maxwell said it best: "In the arithmetic of appetite, anything multiplied by zero still totals zero!"[1]

★

THINK YOUR WAY OUT OF FEAR

A friend of mine was driving down a dark, thickly wooded, unfamiliar road in New England late one weekday night. There were no other cars, and he could only see what his high beams illuminated. As a result, he was moving at the speed limit of thirty-five miles per hour, maybe even below. That's when he learned what the expression "deer trapped in the headlights" literally looks like. As he hit a straightaway, he saw the stag jump into the road, turn its head toward his car, and freeze.

My friend slammed on the brakes and skidded to a stop about two feet from the animal. The animal still stood frozen in front of his car, not moving. It remained that way for minutes as my friend regained his composure. Finally, he honked the horn, and the deer ran off into the night.

Fear makes us freeze in an effort to avoid impending consequences. When we cave to our fears, it often leads to more pain. Sometimes things turn out OK anyway, as they did for that deer and my friend, and we wonder afterward why we were so afraid. Many times, they do not. Most deer are killed or mortally wounded by freezing in fear. Many more are killed or injured because the driver was too scared to react as my friend did. Do not listen to your fears. Do not freeze. It only makes bleak situations worse.

Let's face it: Few of us will face decisions in business that require split-second reactions. There is always time in any situation, no matter how big a crisis you make it (or it really is), to stop and think about what you are thinking. Consider how what you're thinking makes you feel. And remember: Succumbing to fear is just like quitting, because it only considers the worst possible outcome. Choose to face and grow through the emotional pain you're feeling. It will pass. Quitting, however, is forever. Instead of caving to your fears, recognize what you are feeling, and begin to think your way out.

continued

If you're stuck in your head thinking about something else, ask yourself, *What is missing?* Consider the best-case scenario and how to creatively fill that void. Once you have come up with the right answer, respond accordingly, regardless of what emotions you might be feeling in the moment. Never let fear into your heart to sap your hope. Instead, courageously act by making yourself accountable to the best course of action. As we live by this truth in the face of fear, we will certainly win the moment.

★

PASSION ISN'T THE POINT; PURPOSE IS

Passion is important, but it's merely a quick burst of energy followed by burnout. Passion may carry you through a moment, and you may even win a few moments motivated by passion. But when the work becomes too hard or if it takes too long, the energy and drive fueled by this emotion will run out, and you will become susceptible to momentary adversity.

Working with purpose gives your work a cause that is bigger than you. There is nothing quite like the long-term, hard, purposeful work created by a cause greater than yourself—something in which you wholeheartedly believe. Purposeful work will govern action in many moments won until the work is done. When you work with purpose, it does not matter how hard the work is or how long it takes. Compensation for the work you do when you do so with purpose matters less. For a life full of fulfillment, choose to work with purpose over passion.

Your passions are about you, whereas your purpose is for all. To be driven by purpose is noble and enduring. It can cast out fear. With purposeful living, we can experience tangible productivity in our lives. We can feel a great sense of accomplishment with endearing relationships built along the way.

THE ONLY THING WE HAVE TO FEAR

At the end of 2008, I was driving to visit with a client in Denver, Colorado, when I received a phone call from a colleague of mine. After some pleasantries, he asked me how long I planned to continue in this dream of mine without any success in sight. My business was teetering at this point. I was *this close* to failure.

Yet that's when it hit me: I had never believed I would fail and still didn't. I knew things were precarious, and my pride had made things worse than they needed to be, but I still believed that as long as I stuck with what I believed in, it would work out. I did not know how long it would take, and I didn't care either. My belief in my dream, though nothing close to the scale of Dr. King's, was nonetheless similar in one way: My need and my faith in my ability to bring it to reality left no room in my mind for fear.

As I thought back to that call, I asked myself, *Why wasn't I afraid?* The answer was that there simply was no room in my brain for me to take counsel from my fears. Fear and courage cannot exist in the human mind at the same time. One cancels the other out. I turned anything close to fear into adrenaline and more positive emotions.

Fear, in and of itself, is an unpleasant human tendency that is rarely felt based on facts. Rather, it's based on assumptions. Some people don't climb mountains because they have a fear of heights, but many more don't do it because they think they won't be able to do it, or that it is dangerous or will cause pain or suffering of some kind. Racism is based on fear—the belief that someone will hurt you in some way just because of the color of their skin. We fear delivering bad news because we "know" we will get anger, disappointment, or grief and therefore lack the courage to tell it like it is.

Simply put, what we fear are consequences—mostly made up— that cause us to worry that we or those we care about will experience pain or harm. We might fight or flee from it sometimes, but this feeling of anxiety concerning an imagined outcome can also cause inaction. With careful preparation and faith in the truth, we can win moments even in the face of fear.

All the tools and skills we have covered so far—embracing optimism, becoming a student of your work, learning to listen, genuinely caring, giving first—are weapons against the fear that prevents us from winning moments, that holds us back from taking the right action or acting at all. Think about musicians who have stage fright: They can have all the tools and skills they need, and fear will still be the great inhibitor. Those musicians will never take the stage and share their gifts with others if they don't overcome that fear.

TAKING CONTROL AWAY FROM FEAR

Situations that call for action happen every day in business, but fear often prevents us not only from acting but also from seeing solutions that create winning moments. For example, a friend of mine, Mitch, owned a marketing company that bought a lot of advertising space and broadcast time from the media. To thank them for their clients' money and as a perk of doing business together, many media outlets provide marketing companies with gifts, like tickets to sporting events. Many agencies turn around and give those perks to their clients, which is a smart way to strengthen the client-agency relationship.

One year, however, one of Mitch's clients asked him *not* to take any perks or gifts from the media. The client felt that it would skew Mitch's judgment and that, as a result, he would not make the best use of the client's marketing dollars. The client made Mitch promise that he would not take media perks as a condition of doing business together.

If you were Mitch, what would you do? You could make the promise, knowing it was impossible to keep, and not let the client know when you received the perks, or you could make the promise to the client and refuse the perks, even though they were standard practice. There was nothing illegal or unethical about them, and my friend felt he would never let any perk skew his judgment.

Neither option sounded good to Mitch, who now believed he had to figure out which was the lesser of two evils. He turned himself in knots over this. He didn't want to be dishonest, but this client was asking for Mitch to pass up a lot of opportunities that might help him retain or win other clients. However, this client was a big fish, and saying no would seriously impact Mitch's bottom line and might cost him his business in the long run. He created doom-and-gloom scenarios in his head.

All Mitch had to do was—without the defensiveness of ego—ask the client why he thought the perks would skew his judgment. If he had taken the time to not panic or let fear control his thinking, he could have realized that no client had ever asked for this before. He could have used his listening skills to ask questions to make an even bigger winning moment. The client might have thought that the tickets were a bribe, not part of the relationship and a thank-you for Mitch's business. More-over, since it was standard practice in the industry, Mitch knew—but maybe the client didn't—that all the other marketing companies got the same perks from the media outlets, so his decisions would be no more skewed than any other company's.

Mitch could thank the client for being open and honest about his concern and tell him that he represented many clients and that media perks were part of the industry. He could explain that the media can-not be stopped from showering ad agencies with gifts, because that's just what they do. Then, he could ask the client what he really wanted. At the end of the day, every business owner wants results. Mitch could promise the client that if he couldn't provide those results, he would fire himself before the client did. That said, if Mitch was able to do as promised and the media threw perks his way, they could go to a game together and celebrate their marketing successes, donate the perks to a charity, or do something nice for someone else by giving away the game tickets.

The first two either-or, no-win options were driven and locked in by fear, which curbed the confidence and creativity required to see the third answer and the best course of action. Fear creates no-win situations in our heads, which is why we tend to sacrifice what we know is right for fear of the impending consequences. And the consequences are almost never as bad as they seem, except when you let fear control you, because that's when you lose yourself and the truth that fuels the purpose of your work.

SERVICE SOLVES PROBLEMS; MONEY COMES LATER

When I was eleven, I lived with my mother in an apartment complex in an unglamorous part of Cottonwood Heights, Utah. That summer, my big brother, Ben, introduced me to Mountain Dew. I was instantly hooked. I believed that I lived on the edge, like the Mountain Dew commercial said, and the Dew became my drink of choice. All I had to do was head down to the soda machine by the outdoor pool at the apartment complex and pop in a couple of quarters.

It didn't take long for my mom to get sick and tired of me jumping off the walls jacked up on the Dew, so she stopped giving me her spare change.

I *needed* my fix. I just wasn't sure how to get it. One day, riding around the complex on my skateboard, I noticed an older woman struggling to throw her trash in the dumpster. I ran over and helped her push the trash bag in. She was grateful and offered to pay me. My mom had taught me well, so I graciously declined, but she insisted. I followed her back across the street and up three flights to her apartment and waited outside. When she finally came back, she handed me a quarter, smiled, and told me that if I wanted to come back a couple days a week, she would pay me a quarter each time I took out the trash for her.

I agreed to the terms, realizing that our agreement equaled one can of delectable Dew each week. As I started down the steps, I stopped as wheels started turning in my head. Most of the renters in our complex had to climb down these stairs with their trash, cross the street to the dumpster, and then cross back and up to their apartments. I immediately started knocking on doors, offering to take out trash for a quarter.

I made $10 in quarters that *day* before I stopped for my first Dew, all because I found a way to serve others to get what I wanted. By making their lives a little easier, I made my own life better. Every success or moment I have won since then happened because I forgot myself and went to work. Of course, today I need money for much more than a soda, but that's about the scale of responsibility in life. In my experience, no matter how big or small what I needed and wanted to do was, I found that as I stayed focused on using my talents to serve others, the money came, almost as a byproduct.

Listen, I know firsthand how scary it can be when you are short on cash, but you have to stop thinking about yourself and what you need or letting fear of whatever might happen drive you. Forget yourself, and start thinking about what others need most. Become the best at solving that problem, and the money will come. Fear is a stifling emotion. It halts progress. Instead of letting that fear swirl inside your head, turn your thoughts outward and begin to serve others.

When my company went under ten years ago and my youngest son was diagnosed with autism, I didn't have to ask myself what I was going to do. I knew what I had to do. I had to find a common problem out there in the marketplace and solve it better than anyone else could. I had no time for fear. To succeed, I needed to do what I have done my whole life—turn outward and serve. Yes, I let my pride get in the way of accepting help, but just because I could not immediately get past that and help myself didn't mean I couldn't help my business help others.

As for that first client, whose call-handling team I trained for free to keep his account active, he is still a client and dear friend today. When I am in need, I know he'll be there because I have been there for him. By serving others, our needs become less important, and, magically, we find ways to overcome obstacles in ways previously unimaginable.

Simply put, by helping others, we help ourselves. The courage to believe that the money will follow the service you provide others always defeats fear.

THINK THUMBS UP, NOT DOWN

My son Isaac got his thumb caught in a hope chest when he was eighteen months old. It was on Christmas Eve, while I was vacuuming one of the bedrooms upstairs. It happened right behind me. The door of the hope chest slammed shut on Isaac's thumb. I looked up at him as his eyes grew big in complete anguish.

I quickly opened the door and got his thumb out of the way. It was hanging only by its skin. I cupped the palm of my hands around his little hand like a ball and picked him up by the waist with my elbows. He rested on my chest as we scrambled to get all the kids in the car and to the hospital.

The only one who did not cry on the way was Isaac. Whether it was shock or bravery, I do not know. What astounded me, however, was the complete look of trust in his eyes as I held him in my arms on the way to the hospital. He knew he was badly hurt. He also seemed to know that I was going to get him the help he needed.

When we arrived at Primary Children's Hospital, there were not many doctors there. It was Christmas Eve, after all. The kids' grandmother soon arrived to take the other kids while we waited to be seen, Isaac patiently resting on my chest. Once we got in an exam room, they tried to insert an IV. Have you ever tried finding a vein in an eighteen-month-old? The nurses clearly hadn't, and that was the first time Isaac cried.

I had to hold him down while he yelled out in excruciating pain as they poked and prodded everywhere. Yet the look of trust never left his face. The pain he endured must have been intense and certainly unfamiliar. Yet in his own way, Isaac seemed to want to comfort me.

The doctor on call arrived just after the IV was successfully placed in Isaac's leg. He washed his hands, put on some gloves, and inspected the severed thumb. He told us that he needed to call in a hand surgeon. Isaac's pain meds were kicking in at this point, which was good, so I slowly released my grip on him while the doctor answered our questions. When we asked if he would be able to save our son's thumb, he said, "We're going to do everything we can." That's not an answer.

When the hand specialist arrived, the first thing he asked was that we leave the room. We were pretty emotional at the time, but we complied. He carried himself with great confidence. His confidence gave us hope that Isaac's thumb was in the best possible hands. We sensed no fear in him or our son. Just as Isaac trusted me because I showed no fear, we trusted the doctor because he showed none either.

After about ten minutes, the hand surgeon came into the waiting room and announced that he was going to attempt to save Isaac's thumb. He would begin the procedure immediately. He also explained that the hard part was not reattaching the thumb. The bone in his thumb was shattered and the artery was mangled badly. If he could not properly suture the artery and maintain blood flow to the severed tissue, he would not be able to save the thumb.

After we said our goodbyes to Isaac, he was rolled out to surgery, and for the first time, I felt afraid. My heart ached. I asked myself over and over how my son would fare without his thumb. Would the loss affect his ability to succeed in general? How could I help in the event that he became self-conscious about it? I wrestled in high school and wondered if he could ever wrestle. I also blamed myself, replaying all of the "if only" scenarios in my head.

After four hours of surgery, the doctor came into the waiting room and explained the situation. Isaac's ulnar artery was very small. Typically, eight sutures are needed to repair a severed ulnar artery. However, the doctor could only fit four. He also had to put two pins in Isaac's thumb to keep it from moving and give the bone a chance to heal. The plan was to put his hand in a cast, give it six weeks, and pray for a miracle.

Fear and worry consumed me over those next six weeks. Isaac? He never knew the fear. He was mostly back to his happy self, playing and enjoying the company of his siblings and cousins on Christmas. I watched him like a hawk to keep him out of trouble, of course. At one point, he fell off the back of a chair to my absolute horror, but he jumped right up again and kept playing. And after six long weeks of waiting to see if his thumb had been saved, we returned to the hospital.

Somehow seeing the hand surgeon again made us feel hopeful. There was a bond between us, having experienced this horrifying ordeal together just six weeks before. He seemed as anxious as we were to know whether the thumb was still alive, and he took Isaac back to the exam room.

About thirty minutes later, the doctor came out with a smile on his face. The tissue in Isaac's thumb had survived, and the bone was healing nicely. It was a miracle. We all knew it as we shared a collective embrace. Words cannot express the gratitude we felt as tears of joy began to flow. Today, Isaac indeed wrestles like his old man, and he shows the same courage on the mat that he did as a toddler.

Looking back, I'm not sure why I was so worried. Scratch that, I am not sure why I wasted so much time on worrying and fearing for Isaac's future. I chose fear but resolved to never let it consume me again. Isaac can do anything—and he would have been able to do anything without his thumb too. So can you. Believe it. And if you come to an obstacle, believe you can overcome it. And if it sets you back, find a new way to attack or get around it. The choice is yours. Don't let your choice be fear.

CHAPTER 10

FREEDOM FROM ENTITLEMENT

My two brothers, three sisters, and I grew up in Fillmore, Utah, a small town about one hundred miles south of Provo. The three boys—Ben (four years older than me), Nathan (two years younger), and I—slept in the same queen-size bed in one room. The three girls—Renee, Rebekah, and Veronica—slept together in an adjacent room. We didn't have much, but we always had food on our table and a roof over our heads. Life was good from our point of view.

My siblings and I did not know how little we had until we started hanging out at our friends' houses. They all had their own rooms in much nicer homes, and their parents had fancy cars. They had their own toys too. There were times when they didn't have to share with *anyone.*

That's when I had a realization: We were poor.

I clung to that thinking until I was nineteen, graduated high school, and moved to Brazil with a small group of equally anxious and nervous kids my age for our two-year church mission.

Being from Utah, the first things I had to adjust to were the oppressive heat and humidity, but they turned out to be nothing compared to the living conditions. For the first five months, I lived with another person in a run-down, one-bedroom "house" in the Aero Porto neigh-borhood of Belo Horizonte.

I vividly remember the day we arrived there. I was used to sharing a room, but at least my house in Fillmore wasn't completely covered with a half inch of moist dirt. The house did have a refrigerator and a kitchen sink, but where was the bathroom? I looked out the back door, where I found another sink and a couple of clotheslines running from our house to a fence about six feet away. I quickly realized that this was where and how I would wash my clothes for the foreseeable future.

But still no bathroom.

Then I noticed a door behind the sink outside. Behind it was a small room with a toilet next to what looked like a showerhead coming from the ceiling. There was a drain in the floor under the showerhead. There was no curtain or anything separating the shower and the toilet. I now understood why my roommate, who had been in Brazil for more than a year, told me it was so important to wear sandals everywhere, especially in the bathroom.

After we cleaned out the floor of the house, we were hungry. There was nothing to cook with, so we went out to the store and bought some eggs, butter, a frying pan, and a spatula. That's when I noticed there was nothing to cook *on*—no stove.

My roommate was prepared. Like in a scene from *MacGyver*, he grabbed an empty coffee can from our backyard, poked holes all around it about an inch from the bottom, pulled a lighter and rubbing alcohol from his bag, and poured some of the alcohol into the bottom of the coffee can. He lit it through one of the holes and placed the frying pan on the can. That's how we made our eggs that first night. It's how we made our breakfast and dinner most days.

The next challenge was learning Portuguese, the official language of Brazil, but I was probably less concerned about that than about the spiders and scorpions. Every morning, we banged our shoes against the ground before putting them on to make sure we didn't get bit or stung. One day, we found a black scorpion on our kitchen floor after coming back from a long day at work.

My feet grew sore every single day in those shoes, walking anywhere from five to ten miles a day in the heat. We didn't have a car, so with the daily bug check and all the walking, I wore out my shoes quickly.

After about a week, I started missing home, realizing how good I had had it and how much I had taken it for granted. I thought I was poor but now could see clearly how fortunate I was. My family was well-off compared to what I saw in Brazil. Growing up, I had always focused on what I didn't have, so I couldn't see all that I *did* have. So what if my friends and their families had two of everything I had none of or had to share? Before I had recognized what I didn't have by seeing their fancy cars and private rooms, I had thought my life was good. And I was right. *You don't need much to be happy; it all depends on your perspective.*

I did not come to this realization all at once. It took almost four months to push through all the emotional turmoil I felt—from my living conditions to homesickness to being a stranger in a strange land—to get over myself and go to work. Once I did that, I learned that happiness is not found in the things we don't have, but in our relationships and the moments we win while living in truth. And once I figured that out, I was never happier in my life. I lived and loved what I was doing for others, which made any and all sacrifice worth it.

Don't get me wrong: Beautiful homes and big appliances—and especially indoor bathrooms—are nice to have, for sure. It's just that we get into trouble when those accessories become things that we "should" or "deserve" to have—that we are "entitled" to.

TO DESERVE IS FOLLY

Whenever we find ourselves feeling entitled, we become more susceptible not only to big negative tendencies like cheating and stealing, but
also to small ones like telling little lies to get what we feel we deserve.
All this does is inflate our egos. Even simply saying, "I deserve what I
have" does this to us; it makes us think we've earned everything on our
own—or shouldn't have to earn it at all.

But nothing worthwhile comes for free. To get where you want to
be in business—and life—you have to build value for those around
you. Instead of believing that you deserve anything this world has to
offer, first place the spotlight of accountability on you and ask yourself these questions:

- ★ Why do I think I am entitled to what others have?

- ★ Am I asking for what I want without rising to the occasion or
  striving to help myself?

- ★ Do I expect it all to come to me?

- ★ Am I showing resilience when I get knocked down and help
  myself get up, rather than expecting others to bail me out?

Those are the same questions we should ask about the jobs we have
and the work we are doing, instead of thinking we deserve something
more than what we have. Why do you think people still come to our
borders looking for the very jobs we complain are not enough as a
path to better lives? I'm not saying those jobs *are* enough for everyone.
I'm saying that mind-set matters as you learn to free yourself from the
tendency of entitlement. We all came with breath in our lungs. We
have already been given much. The world owes you nothing. We *deserve*
nothing; the chance to live well comes from hard work—blood, sweat,
tears, and a little luck—sometimes a lot of luck.

★

FREELY FORGIVEN

Back in high school, I got a job frying chicken and potato wedges in the back of a local gas station. It was fun, and I could eat all the chicken I wanted. I sometimes worked the register when it got busy, and when it was slow, I would restock the shelves and clean the bathrooms. In time, as I became comfortable in my position, I began to slack off a little. There were video games in the back, and I would often play them when it was slow instead of working.

One day, as I was playing, my boss showed up and sat at a table behind me. He called out my name, to which I yelled back, "I'll be there in a minute," thinking it was just my coworker in the front. About thirty seconds later, my boss called out my name again. This time I recognized the voice and slowly turned around to confirm the alarm going off in my head.

There he was, sitting quietly and patiently at the table. He softly asked me to sit across from him as he motioned in that direction with his right hand. As I approached the bench, I couldn't help but notice that he was more disappointed than angry. When I settled into my seat, he told me I was fired.

I pleaded for him to reconsider. I explained how my dad would kill me when he found out and promised him that if he gave me the opportunity to stay, I would show I could change and become the best worker he ever had. My boss sat there in silence as I repeated, "Please. Please do not fire me. Please."

Most leaders have been in this situation, and if it were our kids across from us and they had betrayed our trust as a parent, we'd totally give them a do-over. But we tend to not be so forgiving outside of the home. I was one of the lucky ones that day.

"All right, Brigham, I'll give you one more shot," my boss said. "But if I catch you back here one more time, that will be the end of it. Understood?"

continued

I agreed to the terms, and he motioned me back to work with his hands. I responded with immense gratitude as I scurried back into the kitchen. I worked there for over a year, until I graduated and left to serve that two-year service mission in Brazil.

When others forgive us, it is a gift. You cannot make someone forgive. It is a miracle given of one's own free will and strength of character. Forgiving yourself is another matter entirely.

You see, forgiveness and letting go do not absolve us from taking responsibility for our actions. There is nothing to forgive ourselves for if we do not fully recognize that what we did was wrong and how we could have done better. Taking steps to correct the wrongs we commit, accepting the consequences of our actions, feeling deep regret and emotional pain of conscience as opposed to feeling sad that we got caught—all are necessary before true penance and self-restitution can come. To truly let go, you must first take responsibility.

Can you let it go? Can you look to the future in the darkest times and believe that your best days are still ahead of you? Can you begin again no matter how old you are (or feel) and how many mistakes you've made? Can you learn from your mistakes and from the mistakes of others?

As long as you are breathing, you can. We can all become better people, and we can do better by others. View your mistakes as opportunities to learn how to win moments and live a more fulfilled life. After all, life in and of itself, as well as your right to choose, are gifts. And what is it that we are doing with these gifts? Multiplying or dividing? Growing or diminishing? Progressing or faltering? As we learn to forgive ourselves and others, our potential for continued multiplicity, growth, and progress in this life have no limits.

★

NO JOB IS A DEAD END

No job we have is a dead end unless we begin to look at it that way. Why do we look down on the nature of certain work and devalue it or the people who do it? I am speaking from experience, because I have done the dirtiest of jobs, from cleaning chicken crap by the shovelful in a mushroom plant to performing various landscaping jobs and laying cement for building foundations. Not one of those opportunities was a waste of my time. They helped shape my character, taught me how to work, and gave me an inner drive to find better ways to provide for myself. This is the less glamorous part of the American dream that gets left out of so many success stories. And there are many stories of people being taken advantage of who are having obstacles put in their way and being conditioned to believe (and thus believing) that there is nothing they can do to change their condition. But that is almost never true. More often, they had something they felt they were entitled to, and it has been taken away or was out of their reach, maybe through no fault of their own. What's most sad to me are salaried workers, often young people who have had all the benefits of a good education and a comfortable upbringing, who complain about their jobs and how they're stuck in them. How you navigate through these feelings shows whether you feel you're entitled to something better or will use your agency to shift your mind-set and work for something better.

I can certainly understand your desire to make more money. However, until others experience your worth, why would they pay you differently? They won't pay for the unproven or the unknown. Can you imagine paying top dollar for a product or service that promises to be of great worth but has never shown as much in any of its beta tests? Not likely. Make it easy by showing others the value you can create first.

That boss who told me not to stretch the truth about the company's services to make a sale? He found me selling cinnamon-roasted almonds in a mall. I hated that job, but I applied myself to the opportunity, and my future boss met me there. He liked the sales pitch I gave him so much that he bought a bag of almonds and offered me that job, opening a new door of opportunity because I created value within my responsibility, whether I liked it or not. Without that job, I would have never had the chance to meet the other mentors who positively affected my life. All from doing my best work, no matter what kind of work that may have been.

If, in your mind, there is no way to move up in your company, and you let that thought negatively affect the way you approach your work, you may find yourself moved out before you have the chance to move up. Stop whining and thinking you are entitled to anything before you ask yourself what you are doing to help your cause. Think about more than yourself, and don't waste time blaming others for your plight. Do the work it takes to get where you want to be, and keep doing it to move up. You must own the role you play, whether you are a leader or on the proverbial bottom rung of the ladder. Then, the way you approach the "game" of work (like life) will determine the outcome.

But remember: To move up, you need to create value for others, no matter what you are doing. By doing so, others can help you get on a more favorable ladder. They will see the value you are creating and will find a way to keep you around, even if that means that they have to change your position. Don't hold your best work in reserve for when you are paid what you feel you are worth. Regardless of your income, give it everything you've got, and show them how amazing you are in the kind of work you are doing.

Don't get me wrong: When people do show that value, companies and their leaders had better step up like my old boss, or they could find themselves losing a valuable employee to their competitor. Value creation is a two-way street, and chances are, if people are delivering value for you, someone else is watching and waiting. If you don't open a door for them, someone else will.

When you embrace this mind-set, you will find that it's not about getting what you "deserve" or what you are "entitled to"; it's about value creation and the volume of people you can help. How many people can you help with the value you create, so you create a mentality of abundance (win-win) rather than scarcity (win-lose)?

You might say that there is no way this kind of abundance mentality could work in such a dog-eat-dog world. Who cares what dogs do? You are not a dog. You are not motivated just by pleasure or pain. Learn to be human or, better put, more humane. *Our humanity is and must be the foundation of who we are. We're not animals, and we cannot act like animals or treat each other like them if we expect to evolve to live by truth.*

Above all else, the dream we are living in this country requires work and self-sacrifice. If that is ever changed and entitlement gets its way, it will spell the end of a dream as well as an era of prosperity.

NO ONE IS AN ISLAND

Entitlement blinds us to what we have, but also to who has contributed to our success. If I say I started my call-handling training business, did the heavy lifting, believed it would work when no one else did, and conceived the ideas that made it grow, it makes it sound like my success is my own, that I deserve what I have because of what I did. But is that true? Some people may think so, but of course it's not true.

For the record, I may run my business, but it is an S Corp, not a sole proprietorship, meaning that there was at least one other person involved in its creation. Sure, in the beginning I did the heavy lifting, such as it is—the call monitoring, training, and coaching—that is, until it became too much for me to handle and I hired help. When I was down, a mentor believed enough in my business and me to pay for the domain name, and my clients believed and invested money in my services. While I can claim many of the ideas implemented in my company, I certainly cannot claim all of them. My success belongs first and foremost to my clients and then to my team; I play a role in that success, but it does not belong solely to me or to my efforts.

It's easy to forget all that when you focus on what you deserve or what you can take for yourself, not what you've been given by others. No one achieves success—no matter how you measure it—completely alone. Our relationships and experiences with others certainly influence our successes. Whether the successful see this truth or not is up to them, but it affects every relationship they have.

This is not to say that you owe any more than what was originally agreed upon between you and those parties that helped you reach the top. Just remember to stay grateful and humble. Don't let your successes change the person you are, or better yet, the person you are working to become.

TRUST IS EARNED, NOT GIVEN

One of my first mentors, John Cooper, was my best friend's dad. He took his son Cole and me horseback riding all the time while I was growing up. When we were with John, he told us stories and put us to work for our rides. I first learned about the birds and the bees when we helped John take his stallions to breed. We shoveled horse crap out of the stalls, washed the horses off, and brushed them down.

John had a deep understanding of his strong but mild-tempered stallions and would not let us ride them without understanding them first. For him, it was a matter of trust.

"Boys," he would say, "with a horse, trust is not given. It is earned. You might be able to get on any horse, but I don't advise it. Because when you're in a pickle, horses will go their own way and do their own thing."

Without trust, he explained, horses would become afraid and unpredictable in difficult situations. This is because horses find *you* unpredictable and untrustworthy. Riding horses without first gaining their trust puts you and the horses at risk. You have to feed, clean, and take care of them. You have to show them that you are a friend and can be trusted. Once you do that, you can ride them anywhere, anytime, and in any condition, and they will listen.

What John taught me about trust through his horses helped me in my relationships throughout my life. You have to give to receive anything, and that includes trust. People, especially your clients and your team, have to be able to trust you if you expect them to stay loyal. When the going gets tough, people can become afraid and unpredictable if they don't trust you. So you have to take care of them. Put their needs before your own. That way, they'll stand by you in any condition. Of course, there are exceptions, but the general rule is simple: *Trust is earned, not given.*

PAY IT FORWARD

Because I have been given much, I, too, should give. Choosing to share your abundant wealth and wisdom with those who need your mentorship is the only way to pay forward what you have been freely given— to give as you have been given. By giving to and serving others, you pay forward what others have done for you.

CHAPTER 11

FREEDOM FROM PRIDE

I went rock climbing one afternoon with my cousins and father-in-law. Training for the Spartan race had elevated my back and finger strength, and everyone watched in awe of and cheered my ability to get up each increasingly difficult wall and make it look so effortless. Although I felt sheepish at first about the applause, the recognition was nice.

After my one climb, my father-in-law, who is in his late sixties, asked if I thought he could do it too. I told him that if he wanted to get up that wall, I would do all I could to make it happen. Heading over to the easiest wall, we got him going, and he struggled at first as he kept trying to pull himself up with his arms. I suggested that he use his legs as much as possible to step up the wall. He needed to let his feet push his hands up. That advice was all he needed to make it to the top. We both felt great about his accomplishment.

Then my cousin stepped up to the wall. She is very athletic, and while she had some experience in rock climbing, she had not done the training I had. But as she succeeded in each climb the way I had, with no advice or help from me, my emotion changed from happy for my father-in-law to something else. As my cousin headed to the hardest wall I had scaled, I was . . . nervous. It had taken all I had to reach the top of that wall.

If she gets to the top of the last one, I thought, *I'm going to have to find a harder wall for us to climb.*

A few feet from the top of the final wall, her fingers lost their grip. She slipped off.

I found myself cheering on the inside, feeling a sense of relief that she didn't make it. That is when it hit me: I felt the way I felt because her successful climb to the top would somehow diminish my success. I already knew what I was feeling at her failure: *schadenfreude,* a feeling of pleasure or satisfaction when something bad happens to someone else. And I felt that way for one reason: my wounded pride.

Pride made me believe that my cousin was undeserving of success that was similar to what I had earned and was entitled to from my training. That same pride had turned a team jog up and down a mountain into a race against my son's wrestling coach. It's the kind of pride that comes when we pit ourselves against others—making everything a competition—and let our egos rule the day. There is nothing wrong with a little healthy competition, and this might have started that way with my cousin. But we tend to make it profoundly unhealthy: I began to wish she would fall so I could feel successful and win a moment that didn't really exist. But I felt only failure and shame as I became aware of what I was feeling.

SOMEONE ELSE WINNING DOESN'T MEAN YOU LOSE

Why shouldn't we endeavor to help others succeed? Why do we sincerely wish for accomplishment by those who pose no threat to our status (my father-in-law on the climbing wall) but turn on those who threaten to overshadow our success instead of working with them to drive each other to even greater heights?

We should wish for each other's accomplishment. We should cheer each other on when we fight to succeed in doing hard things. Sure, we must believe we can win every time, but ultimately we know we can't and that almost every record will eventually be broken. So we should just learn to be as happy when others win, especially when they fought hard and did their best. And when we reach the top, we should never forget to pull others up with us. Don't forget what Zig Ziglar said: You will get all you want in life if you help enough other people get what they want.

In the end, pride only causes destruction. It sends out pessimism and negativity toward others and closes us down to their success. I was completely willing to impart the knowledge I had to my father-in-law as he started his climb, and he was willing to receive it. We both put aside our pride and were mutually invested in his success. It's always easier for us to receive counsel from others when we put aside our pride. We avoid becoming defensive, especially when others are giving us feedback, and we actually listen. But I made no such effort to help my cousin (even though she didn't need it).

The proud spend a lot of time thinking about themselves, and when you focus too much on yourself, you will inevitably let others down. This same pride can easily escalate into rationalizing and justifying the grosser human tendencies, such as deception and fault finding, as a means to an end.

Maybe this way we are no different than animals. You have heard the expression "a wounded animal is the most dangerous animal," but they don't have to be literally wounded to be dangerous. An animal that feels trapped is equally dangerous and will lash out because it thinks everything and everyone is trying to hurt it. That's what pride does to humans when someone or something makes our accomplishments or us feel "less than." That's when enmity creeps in and pride becomes dangerous.

FAITH AND MOMENTS OF TRUTH

On November 16, 2010, I wrote myself a letter just after boarding a plane to New York City and called it the "Hail Mary Pass." As you might have inferred from my name, I am a huge Brigham Young University (BYU) football fan, and the Hail Mary Pass is legend at BYU. The Hail Mary is a desperation long throw for the end zone when there are only a few seconds remaining, and the moment of truth—victory or defeat—hangs in the balance. One of the greatest comebacks in sports history came when BYU quarterback Jim McMahon completed a Hail Mary Pass in the 1980 Holiday Bowl, and in 1984 we won the national championship with a shorter version of the pass with a minute to go.

That's what this trip felt like for me: a moment of truth. Family, friends, business associates—all of them had asked me to put a stop to this "charade" of a start-up I was working on. It would never work, they said. And now I was putting money I did not have on a credit card that I already owed money on to spend days trying to close business for a venture that was sure to fail. "At what point should you get a job?" they all asked me. Part of me couldn't help but listen and ask myself, *Are they right?* They had been supportive when I started but now had turned on me. I thus decided that my trip to New York was it. I had better get at least one of the three potential clients in the area to sign or I would start sending around my resume in Utah.

This was my Hail Mary Pass.

I wrote the letter to remind myself I still had this chance. I still believed in me and what I was doing. Was the decision to fly to New York risky? Of course. The biggest potential lay in a client meeting I had scheduled based on a discussion I had with an employee there, but I had an appointment with the owner now because of it. Whether I would beat the odds and close this sale or not was irrelevant. What mattered is that I was going and doing what I felt I was supposed to do and believed in my ability to seize this opportunity—to make this moment happen and win it.

The meeting was a bust. I waited for over an hour before the owner showed up, and he was running late for his appointment after mine. He graciously gave me five minutes for making the trip to explain what I could do for him and his team. I did the best I could to leave an impression.

But instead of hanging my head, I headed to New Jersey for another meeting I had set up and ended up spending an hour with the general manager. He liked what I said, but in the end, he was not ready to move forward with what I had in mind.

So I headed back across a bridge to Staten Island for my final opportunity. That meeting was good too. We connected well, but I soon realized that I was not talking to the decision maker. I was frustrated with myself because I knew better. I could hear the words of übersalesman Jeff Gitomer echoing in my head: "You suck."

I felt pretty down. Then I hit a new low when I called home to report my losses.

I didn't sleep well and was up early to pack my bag for the trip home. In the hours between my final meeting the day before and getting ready to check out, I evaluated my performance in the meetings. I thought about what I should have done differently. I thought about my promise to give it up when I got home if I failed. Suddenly, I remembered how important this trip was and how confident I previously felt that I could make something happen. Could I still make something happen? I wasn't home yet. My flight didn't leave until the afternoon. I still had time to call each of the companies I had visited the day before for a gentle nudge.

The owner in New York was not available. Shocker there.

The employee in Staten Island gave me the real boss's phone number, and we scheduled a conference call for the following week, which was great. Maybe I had more time on the clock.

continued

Finally I called the general manager in New Jersey, and we talked for a little bit before he asked if I had time to come back into his office. We met and negotiated an agreement, at which point he signed on the dotted line. Touchdown!

On November 19, after my trip home, I wrote on the bottom left-hand corner of the Hail Mary Pass letter: "I made a sale. If BYU can do it, so can I." Three opportunities that were more like prayers than anything else turned into the beginning of my company's success. That one account opened the door to over ten accounts nationwide. During the following months, the prospective client in Staten Island signed up too. *Faith can work to create serendipity for you if it is supposed to, but only if you believe and are willing to work toward what is possible. If you believe it can happen, it can!*

Remember: To win moments, you *must* positively act on your belief. The future is only as bright as your faith. Believe in your capacity to learn, grow, and succeed. Think big and let the work *work* for you. If it is supposed to happen, it will—if you continue to move forward and act upon your faith. And if it doesn't, learn to forgive yourself and then to forgive others for any trespasses against you, no matter how devastating.

★

HOW DO WE AVOID BECOMING PROUD?

The cure for all of this is to do more thinking about others and their needs. And the easiest way is to recognize others for the role they play in your success or the accomplishments they achieve with their own hard work. Congratulations and sincere expressions of gratitude are gifts to others that cost nothing and, when heartfelt and given freely and genuinely without any expectation of anything in return, break us free from the cyclical nature of pride. *When was the last time, as Ken Blanchard famously said, you caught someone doing something right?*

I use the word *cyclical* because the trouble with pride occurs when we inhale our successes, which makes us feel puffed up and self-absorbed. While in this state, it alienates us from others. We become competitive, appreciating compliments and accolades directed toward us while feeling enmity about the accomplishments of others. We seek to self-elevate. And we often at least hope for the demise of others. We do not recognize it in the moment, of course. In our prideful state, everyone else is playing a supportive role in our world.

In this life, we are in competition with no one other than ourselves. Our tendencies are the enemy. They keep us from being great. They keep us from living what is true, from winning moments, and from living a life patterned after excellence. My challenge to you is to learn to win the moment by breaking pride's cycle and choosing to remain completely grateful for the opportunity to serve. Consider what you do for others as a stewardship—an opportunity to serve them, an opportunity you can lose at any time if you become overly self-absorbed or self-elevated. It's time to forget yourself and go to work in the service of your fellow beings.

CHAPTER 12

HOLD TRUE TO THE TRUTH

At the end of a wrestling tournament, my son Isaac came off the mat with a look of disappointment, dropped his headgear to the ground, and fell into my arms, sobbing.

"I am so sick of losing," he said.

"Son, it is not about winning or losing matches. It's about getting better. Every time you step on the mat, win or lose, choose to learn from it, to be better for it, regardless of the outcome. Every minute on the mat is a minute of experience that will make you better than you were before, if you let it. Let each match make you better, and don't you ever quit."

As I finished, I realized I was talking as much to myself as I was to Isaac. The moments we find ourselves in are very much like my son's wrestling matches.

As long as we are living, we can *choose* to get up when we fall. *Choose* to learn from each moment, win or lose. Lost moments do not have to define us, as long as we *choose* to let those losses change us and become better than we were before. One of the greatest things about life is that we can fall forward. Because we are human, we all make mistakes, and our tendencies will get the best of us from time to time. When we choose to learn from a fall, then in that sense we fall forward, and we become better for it.

It doesn't matter if we win or lose the moment. What makes us winners and losers is what comes next. That's the rest of what I told Isaac that day: "When you start winning more matches—and you will as long as you work hard and keep at it—don't forget how it feels to lose. When you win, the other guy you just wrestled lost. Help him up. Embrace him and share words of encouragement. Never forget how it feels and let that motivate you to work hard with a desire to inspire others to follow the example you have set for them."

As I sat there on the edge of the mat consoling my boy, we talked about the wrestlers he'd known who quit coming to practice because it was too hard. They never had a moment to win or lose. They were unwilling to pay the price to progress, and they succumbed to the worst human tendency of all: quitting because, from their point of view, it was just too hard, too much work to keep going.

Whether you endeavor to perform athletically or interpersonally in moments of truth, you can't win—you can't *do*—unless you choose to try and keep trying until your ability is perfected. So try until trying becomes doing. And you'll soon find that doing is not enough either: You must *be*. When we live by what is universally true, consequentially, we not only win in pivotal moments and keep winning them, but also experience the most important thing that comes with them: inner peace. It sounds a little corny, but when you choose to do what is right over what is easy, you free your conscience of the impending guilt that comes when you choose to do wrong. Shrinking to our tendencies causes inner turmoil, impedes our progress, and makes us miserable.

CLIMB OUT OF THE BUCKET

Misery loves company, but that doesn't mean you have to *be* that company. Those metaphorical crabs we discussed earlier pull each other down so no one crab can escape the bucket. Each of us is one of those crabs at some point, when we think we're not smart enough, not strong enough, or not good enough. That is the enemy within—our ego— holding us back. It is so much easier to justify repeatedly shrinking to human tendency when everyone else around us is doing it—and to keep that cycle repeating by pulling everyone around us down. Human tendency makes us captive when we yield to it. The freest people in the world are those who choose to live by truth rather than to shrink to tendency.

Will living by truth lead to wins every time we take to the mat? Of course not! There will certainly continue to be bumps in the road and challenges to overcome. They will hurt too. Peaks and valleys are part of life. Discipline yourself to stay focused on doing right while in a moment, no matter what! Remember: The more moments we win, the freer we become.

But the truth alone does not liberate us; only when we actively seek to discover and *apply it* in our lives—only when we *act* on it—do we win moments and experience real and lasting contentment. As long as you hold true to the truth, no outside force or commotion in the world can stop you. Even when you lose an inner battle, succumbing to tendency, holding true to what you know will ultimately win you the war.

Living by truth is easy when you think about the results. When you're able to see the bigger picture and act on what is most important, you move beyond the tug and pull of human tendency and into true agency. At the end of the day, applied truth is simply the application of sound reasoning over your emotional reactions. All we need to do is think about what we're thinking while in a moment, imagine the best possible outcome, and act accordingly. Pay attention to how you feel.

Be sick of losing! Own that feeling, let it in, and learn from it. Consider what is possible. Do not limit yourself. Do not settle.

THE FORTIFY FIVE

Consider all we have covered in this book: When negativity overtakes optimism. When self-confidence morphs into ego. When we forget to listen. When caring fails in indifference. When we seek to take for ourselves instead of giving first. When fear sets in and saps our courage. When we feel entitled instead of pushing forward to create value for others. When we choose enmity and pride as opposed to being grateful. When we get caught unaware in a moment of truth and shrink before we even know what happened.

I have five simple guidelines to help you fortify yourself on the path to living by truth. I call these the Fortify Five:

(Have) Faith

You must have faith in your capacity to overcome obstacles and learn to grow from moments both won and lost. You need to believe in yourself and your ability to do whatever you set your mind to doing—that you can begin anew no matter how many times you lose, how far you have fallen, or how bad you think you might be. As long as there is breath in your lungs, you can get up, dust yourself off, and try again to live by truth.

Forgive

Forgiveness starts with accepting that you as well as everyone around you are human and fallible, subject to shrinking and succumbing to human tendencies. Past performance, no matter how lackluster or bleak it may be, does not define us and hold us back from moving forward unless we *choose to let it* because of an unwillingness to learn from it or choose not to forgive a past transgression. The key is not necessarily to forget, but to *forgive*. The past does not make us who we are, as long as we *choose* to grow through it and to be something different than we were before. We all have agency—the ability to act as opposed to being acted upon. Remember: We are not toasters! We can learn. We can let go of the past. We can learn to forgive.

(Become a) Founder

When you push through the impeding consequences of previous actions and are able to cut yourself and others a little slack, to move forward and start anew, you become a founder—the master of your fate. This is what makes you heroic—when you take human agency to a whole new level, realizing that you are the author of your own life. This is how you become the person you want to be over time, independently of circumstance and events as they occur. You can envision and create your ideal you no matter how many moments you have lost. Just make a choice and commit that from this day forward, you will live by the truth no matter what challenge comes your way. You will start anew, always striving to be the founder of your life. You are the hero in your story because you refuse to yield to your tendencies.

Feel

Once you become the founder, the next step is to recognize how you feel while in a moment and learn to discern human emotion from truth. Your intuition is more powerful than your intellect. Becoming aware of how you feel in a moment and deciphering it from your instinctive, reactionary emotions gives you an incredible advantage over others who cannot. These feelings—whether they speak peace to your mind, warmth to your soul, sudden clarity in obscurity or confusion, or an increase of indescribable love felt—must be attended to. If you are not quiet and paying attention when they occur, they will come and go unnoticed. These feelings or impressions are not mild expressions. Rather, they are pure intelligence being poured into your mind. And there will certainly be times when the discovery of a truth cuts you to the very center, painfully severing pride from your soul. Learn to become sensitive to the understanding that comes when you experience these feelings, because important personal change is underway. These impressions will educate your desires, which can work affirmatively in you and for you, for your good and the good of others.

Finish

Choose to let these moments of clarity propel you to be a finisher, meaning to live determined to complete what you start no matter what it takes. No matter how hard it might be to live the truth you know, to never quit, to learn, to grow. To become better than the you *you* currently are! Remember: Shrinking to human tendency is the norm. There is nothing unique about it. Do not sell out to mediocrity. There is no lasting happiness there. There never was and there never will be. Only when you choose to rise in truth will you stand out and become truly heroic during life's pivotal moments. So, get up when you fall, dust yourself off, and finish!

ARE YOU LIVING BY TRUTH?

Our bodies, the air we breathe, and our right to choose are gifts. And we live in a time of great freedom and prosperity, with technological advances such as indoor plumbing, heating and air-conditioning, and the internet. Since the beginning of recorded history, there has never been a more advantageous time than now. What are you doing with all the gifts you have been given?

Do you maintain an optimistic outlook on life? Do you remain hungry in your learning, always working to increase your capacity to do anything you set your mind to doing? Or do you let momentary failure or success give way to progress-impeding ego? Do you listen to your life's lessons and learn from them, or do you forget, struggling through the same battles over and over again? Do you care about others, or are you stuck in selfishness—only caring about yourself? Do you give of your talents and time in the service of others, or do you only seek to take from others? Are you a helpless bystander, overcome by fear in a moment, or do you courageously take action? Are you foolish enough to believe that you deserve anything more than what you have already been given without expending your blood, sweat, and tears, or are you willing to put in the hard work necessary to make more out of what you have been given? Have you put off the pride in your heart by recognizing how lucky you are?

To look at your life with anything less than total gratitude today would be like declaring famine in a grocery store. We are meant to grow, to build, to learn, and to earn. Tremendous good can come into our world when we consider the needs of our neighbors as much as or even more than our own and actively engage in meeting those needs. Creating the best version of ourselves while making life a little easier for everyone else around us is what leads to winning moments.

It is not too late for you to begin living by truth over tendency. As long as you have a heart beating in your chest, you can exercise your agency to begin choosing what is right over what is easy. Do not delay progress in your life any further. Today is the day to recognize and righteously act on moments.

Real happiness and the daily application of what is universally true are inseparably connected. This is the road less traveled, and the most free people in the world are on it. Let this truth make you truly free as you choose now to live your life patterned after excellence.

NOTES

CHAPTER 1

1. Sinek, Simon. "InfusionCon." Speech. InfusionCon, Phoenix Convention Center, Phoenix, AZ, April 2014.

CHAPTER 2

1. Uhlig, Daria Kelly. "What Is Touchpoint Marketing?" Small Business–Chron.com. November 21, 2017. https://smallbusiness.chron.com/touchpoint-marketing-34078. html (retrieved March 20, 2019).

CHAPTER 4

1. Cameron, Kim. "Five Keys to Flourishing in Trying Times." *Leader to Leader*, no. 55 (2010): 45–51. doi:10.1002/ltl.401.2.

2. Ianzito, Christina. "Oldest Yoga Teacher Shares Life Lessons." AARP. November 7, 2016. https://www.aarp.org/health/healthy-living/info-2016/yoga-worlds-oldest-teacher .html (retrieved March 20, 2019).

CHAPTER 5

1. "It's Time to Give Noel Burch Some Credit." Exceptional Leaders Lab. July 11, 2017. http://exceptionalleaderslab.com/its-time-to-give-noel-burch-some-credit (retrieved March 20, 2019).

CHAPTER 6

1. "A Message from Your Brain: I'm Not Good at Remembering What I Hear." *National Geographic*. May 17, 2016. https://news.nationalgeographic.com/news/2014/03/140312 -auditory-memory-visual-learning-brain-research-science (retrieved March 20, 2019).

CHAPTER 7

1. Maravelas, Anna. *How to Reduce Workplace Conflict and Stress: How Leaders and Their Employees Can Protect Their Sanity and Productivity from Tension and Turf Wars*. Franklin Lakes, NJ: Career Press, 2005.

2. "Executive Coaching Qualifications | Churchill Leadership Group." Churchill Leadership Group Inc. https://www.churchillleadershipgroup.com/our-qualifications (retrieved March 20, 2019).

3. Culbert, Samuel A., and John B. Ullmen. *Don't Kill the Bosses! Escaping the Hierarchy Trap*. Oakland, CA: Berrett-Koehler, 2001.

4. Culbert, Samuel A., and Larry Rout. *Get Rid of the Performance Review: How Companies Can Stop Intimidating, Start Managing—and Focus on What Really Matters*. New York: Grand Central Publishing, 2010.

5. Covey, Johnny, and Ken Shelton. *5 Habits to Lead from Your Heart: Getting Out of Your Head to Express Your Heart*. Issaquah, WA: Made for Success Publishing, 2016.

6. "Mother Teresa." Wikipedia. March 16, 2019. https://en.wikipedia.org/wiki/ Mother_Teresa (accessed March 19, 2019).

CHAPTER 8

1. Kruse, Kevin. "Zig Ziglar: 10 Quotes That Can Change Your Life." *Forbes*. July 8, 2013. https://www.forbes.com/sites/kevinkruse/2012/11/28/zig-ziglar-10-quotes-that -can-change-your-life/#6003912826a0 (retrieved March 19, 2019).

CHAPTER 9

1. Maxwell, Neal A. "'Repent of [Our] Selfishness' (D&C 56:8)." Neal A. Maxwell. https://www.lds.org/general-conference/1999/04/repent-of-our-selfishness-d-c-56 -8?lang=eng (retrieved March 19, 2019).

INDEX

B righam Dickinson is President of Power Selling Pros, the company that powers your customer experience with CSR certification for literally thousands of call handlers in our industry, PowerTech training services in contractor shops all over the country, and customer retention tools that keep your customers coming back to buy from you more often! He is also the founder of Power Certification, a coaching and training program that holds teams accountable to creating WOW! Experiences over the phone as well as in the customers' home. Brigham started Power Selling Pros over ten years ago when he saw that call handlers needed assistance consistently converting calls to bookings. As a result, he answered the need and created Power Certification to effect change in our industry's call centers all over the world. This program guarantees that contractor call-handling teams will book at least 85% of their calls and WOW more customers. Today, Power Selling Pros holds your office and field staff accountable with a combination of in-person group training, one-on-one phone-based coaching, online course training, and pre-recorded call-monitoring, all supported by a vast library of online training videos that showcase industry best practices. The purpose of the Power Certification Program is to partner with contractors and train their office and field staff to consistently deliver a world class customer experience that is custom built by design at every customer touch point. Power your customer experience with Power Selling Pros.